TAROT
FOR
ENTRE
PRENEURS

ALSO BY MARIËLLE S. SMITH

52 Weeks of Writing Author Journal and Planner, Vol. I: Get out of your own way and become the writer you're meant to be

52 Weeks of Writing Author Journal and Planner, Vol. II: Get out of your own way and become the writer you're meant to be

52 Weeks of Writing Author Journal and Planner, Vol. III: Get out of your own way and become the writer you're meant to be

365 Days of Gratitude Journal: Commit to the life-changing power of gratitude by creating a sustainable practice

365 Days of Gratitude Journal, Vol. II: Commit to the life-changing power of gratitude by creating a sustainable practice

Fleshing Out the Narrative: A 31-Day Tarot and Journal Challenge for Writers

Get Out of Your Own Way: A 31-Day Tarot Challenge for Writers and Other Creatives

Set Yourself Up for Success: A 31-Day Tarot Challenge for Writers and Other Creatives

Seven Simple Spreads 1: Seven Simple Card Spreads to Unlock Your Creative Flow

Seven Simple Spreads 2: Seven Simple Card Spreads to Direct Your Creative Flow

Seven Simple Spreads 3: Seven Simple Card Spreads to Boost Your Confidence

Seven Simple Spreads 4: Seven Simple Card Spreads to Celebrate Your Creative Wins

Speak Your Truth: A 31-Day Tarot Challenge for Writers and Other Creatives

Step into Your Power: A 31-Day Tarot Challenge to Unleash Your Creative Potential

Tarot for Creatives: 21 Tarot Spreads to (Re)Connect to Your Intuition and Ignite that Creative Spark

CO-WRITTEN UNDER THE PEN NAME HEATHER MACLEE

Too Good to Be True?

Where There's a Will

There's a Way

TAROT

FOR

ENTRE

PRENEURS

50 tarot spreads
and other intentional practices
to build your business and tackle its
challenges from the heart

Mariëlle S. Smith

ISBN 978 94 93250 60 4

How you climb a mountain
is more important than
reaching the top.

Yvon Chouinard

TABLE OF CONTENTS

INTRODUCTION

Welcome to *Tarot for Entrepreneurs*, a book featuring fifty tarot spreads and other intentional practices to help entrepreneurs build their business and tackle its challenges from the heart.

Tarot for Entrepreneurs contains a wide variety of spreads, including ones on your strengths and weaknesses, your money story and how to change it, your ideal audience, what to delegate and prioritise, when and how to level up, where to go next, when to quit, how to sell yourself without selling your soul, how to say 'No', and more.

Besides fifty full card spreads, *Tarot for Entrepreneurs* also includes a selection of one-, two-, and three-card spreads and a handful of other intentional practices that will help big and small business owners centre themselves and connect to their inner guidance. You will find these additional sections at the end of the book.

Although I dubbed the card spreads in this book tarot spreads, there is no reason why you shouldn't use any other means of divination to work with them. Feel free to pick your favourite oracle deck or set of angel cards or to use your crystals or runes when working with this book. If you want to mix it up as you do a reading, go ahead. Your gut will tell you what works best for you; don't be afraid to listen.

Cartomancy as a tool to (re)connect to our intuition

Those who are familiar with my work know that I don't merely see cartomancy as a means for divining the future. Throughout my cardslinging career, I've used the card decks at my disposal first and foremost as tools to (re)connect to my intuition.

I do ask questions about the future – from the most probable outcome if I do X or Y to what a particular project might bring me – but I still mostly sling cards to understand what is going on in this exact moment: 'What is going on with me right now?' 'What could I be doing (differently) right now?' 'What do I need to know about the situation I am in right now?'

In other words, I tend to use my cards to become mindful of the moment, tune in to my intuition, and figure out where I truly stand in relation to whatever it is I'm asking questions about.

We already know everything there is to know; we have simply forgotten that we do. From a very young age onwards, most of us were taught to disregard this inner knowing – and not just by our parents, our teachers, and our peers. Most societies are anything but accommodating when it comes to those who like to take the time to sit with themselves, reflect on what they've been told about the world and their roles within it, and listen intently to what is true for their own selves on the most personal and sacred of levels.

Frankly, most societal structures are built in such a way that there is precious little time to ask whether we'd like to do things differently and unlearn everything we think we know so that we can return to what we've always already known on that deeper level. Why? Because the world would not look the way it does now if we were all aligned with our inner knowing and acted on it. There would be little room for greed, harm, oppression, inequality, and inequity if all humans were attuned to their intuition.

Bypassing the ego

That we've learned to disregard our intuition and disconnect from it doesn't mean none of the messages get through. They do. Depending on how far removed we are from our inner knowing, we might hear our inner voice more or less often, louder or less loud, but it does speak to us. The challenge is that these intuitive nudges are exactly the kind of messages most of us were taught to second-guess. After all, they can sound far from rational. This is how we've ended up ignoring our most inner wisdom, that deep knowing that wants nothing but to guide us.

When you suppress and deny your intuition again and again, it becomes harder each time to tune back in. That's where the cards come in for me. My cards hardly ever tell me something I wasn't already aware of on some level. If they do, it's because I'm not ready to realise something yet or too stubborn to hear the message. It happens, and more often than you might think.

What my cards do provide me with are answers to the following question: 'Which of the different messages racing around in my head right now are actually my own?' They help me differentiate between what I think I know – because I was told to believe so by others – and what I actually know deep inside of me. As such, cards – and the same goes for other methods of divination – are a tool to bypass the ego and everything else that stands between us and that voice within us that simply *knows*.

It is for this purpose that I wrote Tarot for Entrepreneurs: to help my fellow entrepreneurs, whether they own a big company or a small one, are freelancers or independent creators, to get and stay as close to themselves as they can be so they can create and maintain heart-centred businesses that radiate their innermost values and beliefs.

No matter what you're struggling with as an entrepreneur, this book will provide you with the right spread to tune (back) in to that inner knowing and make business decisions that are fully aligned with who you are and who you want to be in the world.

Seven sections + one

For the sake of useability and coherence, I divided the card spreads in this book amongst seven sections: Start, Succeed, Sustain, (be) Sovereign, Switch, Stretch, and Stop. Due to the success of the Kickstarter campaign I ran to finance the creation of this book and its companion card deck, The Sovereign Success Oracle, an eighth section was added – Staple – to include all the card spreads that were unlocked during the campaign.

While I tried to categorise the spreads the best I could, the sections are not a perfect fit. This isn't due to the sections themselves. First, most of the card spreads in this book transcend the section I put them in and touch upon the other themes as well. The reason they were placed in their sections is because those made the most sense to me, both logically and intuitively.

Second, while the seven main sections present a sort of timeline – from starting up to stopping – life is far from linear. As frustrating as it is, we tend to come back to the same struggles and challenges over and over. I've lost count of the many times I've asked myself, 'I thought you figured that one out already?' What does change is that, if we learn (some of) the lessons we had to face during the previous cycles, we will be better equipped to deal with whatever comes up for us during the next cycle and able to go deeper. As such, it's my assumption that each section will have something to offer you somewhere along the way, no matter where you are on your entrepreneurial journey.

Make this book your own

As I already mentioned at the start of this introduction, I strongly encourage you to use whatever divination tool you're comfortable with, whether that means the tarot, oracle or angel cards, runes, crystals, a combination of all the above, or something else altogether. I will use whichever card deck of mine feels right in the moment when I do a reading.

Whether you're new to cartomancy or you've been slinging cards for decades, some spreads might seem overwhelming, perhaps because of their size or the questions asked. If that's the case, you should feel absolutely free to disregard the questions you don't need or want an answer to right now. If you're only seeking the answer to one or two of the questions in any given spread, I'd be the last person stopping you from giving yourself a one- or two-card reading using those very questions.

Likewise, if a question doesn't entirely speak to you, do reformulate it in a way that does work for you. The same goes for the order of the cards. If another order makes more sense to you, shake it up. The other intentional practices I included here can be treated in the exact same way. Keep what you like, change what you don't, and take it from there. The only intention I have ever had with any of my books is to unlock people and set them free, so please, don't let yourself be limited by anything in this book in any way.

Start

Whether you're at the outset of your entrepreneurial journey or about to begin a new project or collaboration, the card spreads in this section will help you set yourself up for success in the best way possible.

1

THE ENTREPRENEUR'S SPREAD

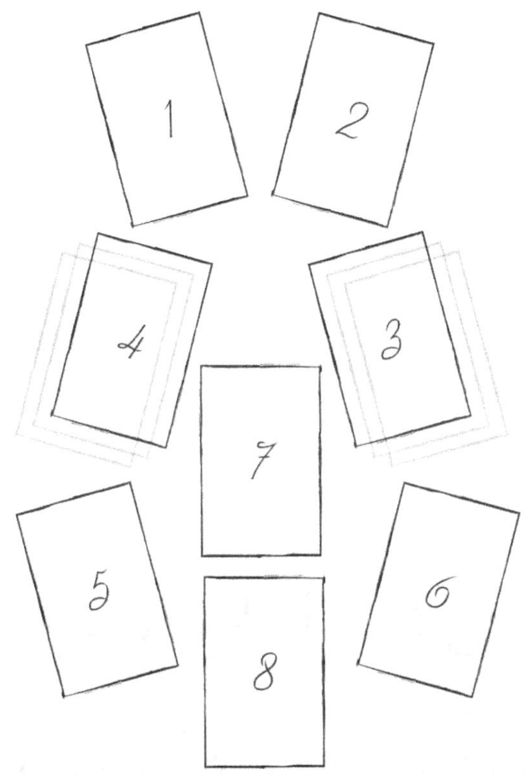

1. Why do I want to be an entrepreneur?

2. What do I love the most about being an entrepreneur?

3. What are my strengths as an entrepreneur?

(Draw up to three cards.)

4. What are my weaknesses as an entrepreneur?

(Draw up to three cards.)

5. What is my biggest struggle as an entrepreneur?

6. How do I overcome this struggle?

7. What do I need to know about my being an entrepreneur?

8. What do I need to know about my entrepreneurship?

2

DO I HAVE WHAT IT TAKES

to be an entrepreneur?

At the very start of our entrepreneurial journey, there's often doubt. Lots of it. Do we have what it takes? Not just to be an entrepreneur but to be a successful one? If you're having any doubts right now, do this spread and see what comes up for you.

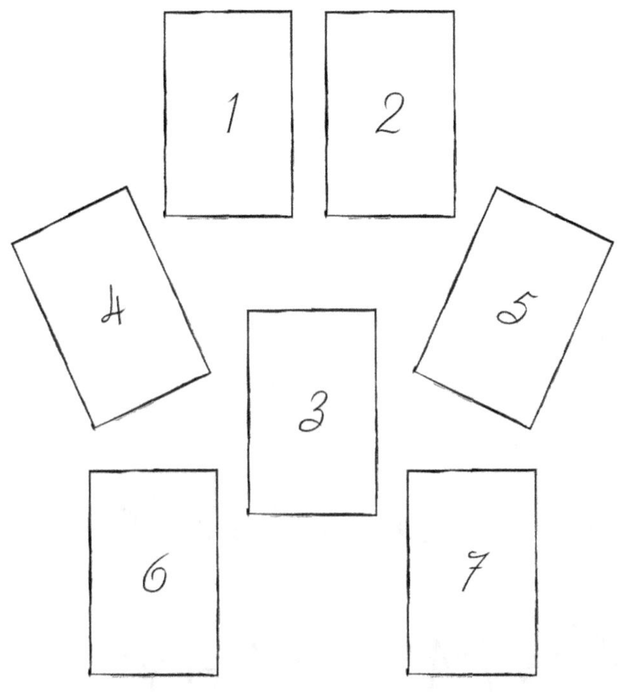

1. What path has led me here?

2. Why did this path lead me here?

3. Why am I doubting whether I have what it takes to be

an entrepreneur?

4. Where does this doubt come from?

5. How can I best overcome this doubt?

6. What do I need to remember about myself right now?

7. What advice do I need to take to heart before taking the leap?

3
KNOWING MY WHY

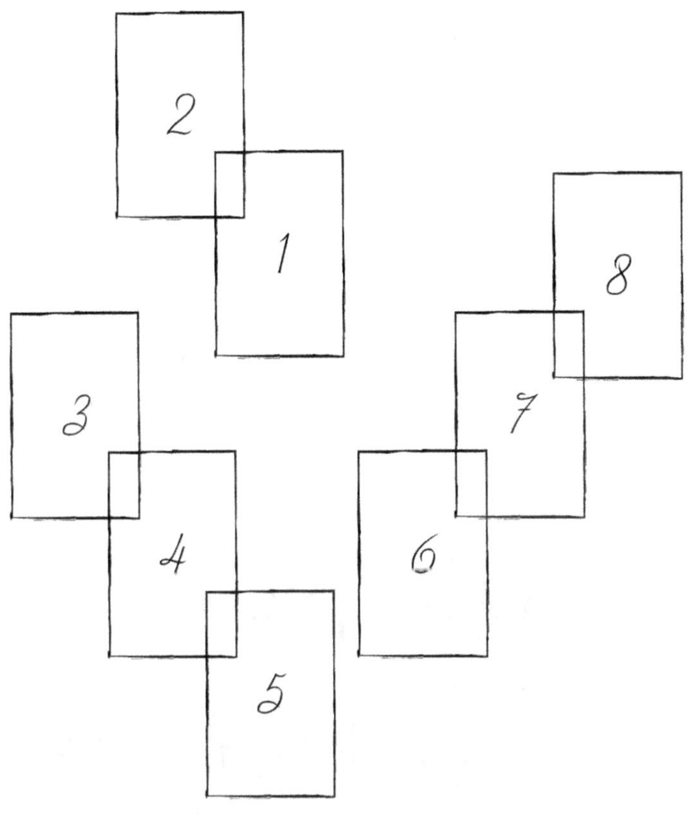

1. Why do I want to start this business?

2. How does this business align with my soul's purpose?

3. What do I want to achieve with this business?

4. Why do I want to achieve this with my business?

5. How can I best align what I want to achieve with my soul's purpose?

6. How do I want to run this business?

7. Why do I want to run my business in this way?

8. How do I stay true to my soul as I run this business?

4

MY IDEAL CLIENT

Getting clear about our ideal client is such a vital and necessary step of being an entrepreneur. This three-part spread will provide clarity on who your ideal client is, why this is so, and where you might find this ideal client of yours.

If you do all three parts of this spread, please remember to write down the results of your draw and return all cards to the deck after each part to shuffle them anew.

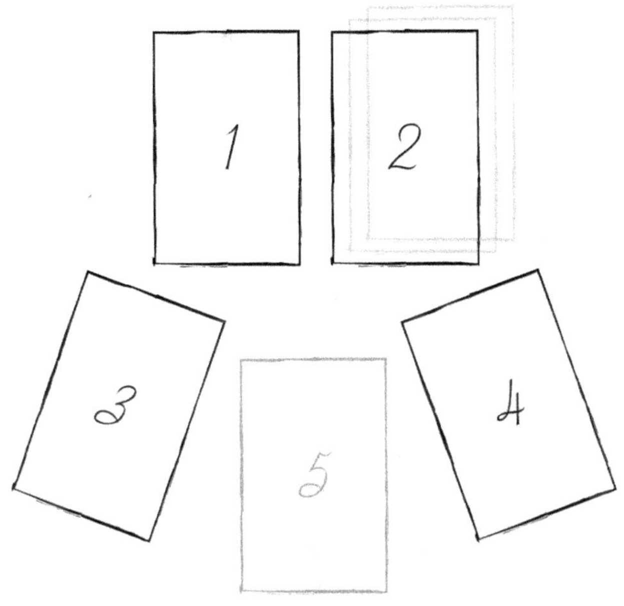

Part 1 – who is my ideal client?

1. What is my ideal client's most obvious or important characteristic?

2. What other characteristics do I need to look out for?

(Draw up to three cards.)

3. What best defines my relationship to my ideal client?

4. What best defines my ideal client's relationship to me?

5. What do I need to remember about working with my ideal client?

(If you're only drawing cards for Part 1, then answer this question now. If, however, you're drawing cards for Parts 1-3, skip this question and ask it after drawing cards for Part 3.)

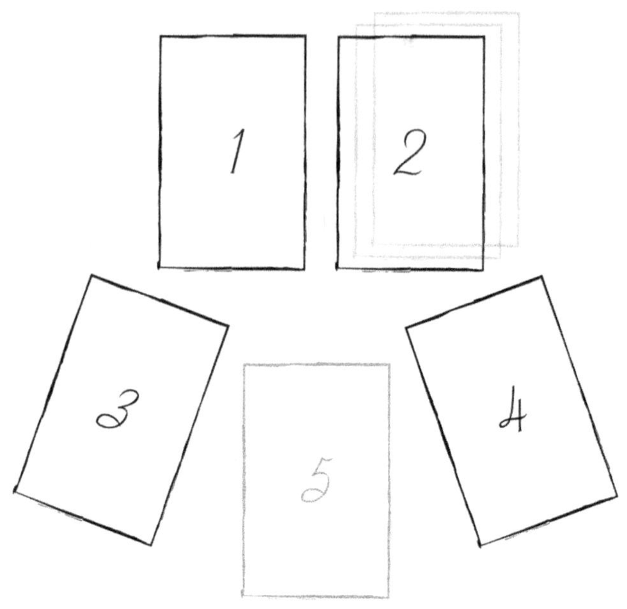

Part 2 – why is this my ideal client?

1. What does my ideal client need from me the most?

2. What else does my ideal client need from me?

(Draw up to three cards.)

3. Why am I the right person to provide my ideal client with this?

4. Knowing this, how can I best help my ideal client?

5. What do I need to remember about working with my ideal client?

(If you're only drawing cards for Part 2, then answer this question now. If, however, you're drawing cards for Parts 1–3, skip this question and ask it after drawing cards for Part 3.)

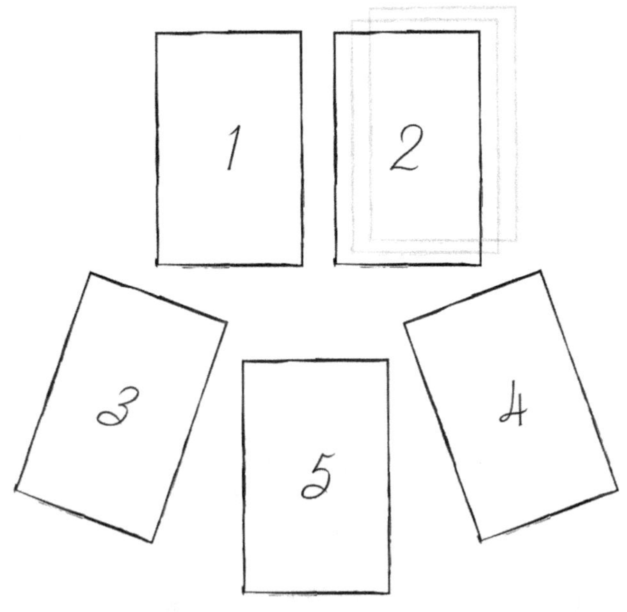

Part 3 – where do I find my ideal client?

1. Where am I the most likely to find my ideal client?

2. Where else might I find my ideal client?

(Draw up to three cards.)

3. How do I attract my ideal client?

4. How do I keep my ideal client?

5. What do I need to remember about working with my ideal client?

5

I HAVE EVERYTHING I NEED

The Magician's spread

Whatever you're getting yourself ready for, this spread will help you take stock of all your strengths, your potential obstacles, and how you can make the most of both on the journey ahead.

If you do all three parts of this spread, please remember to write down the results of your draw and return all cards to the deck after each part to shuffle them anew.

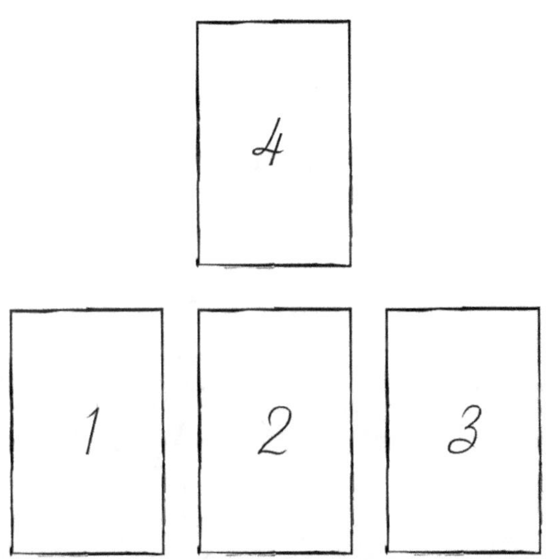

Part 1 – my strengths

1. What needed strength am I the most comfortable with?

2. What needed strength am I the least comfortable with?

3. What needed strength am I forgetting about?

4. What about these strengths will prove to be the most

useful here?

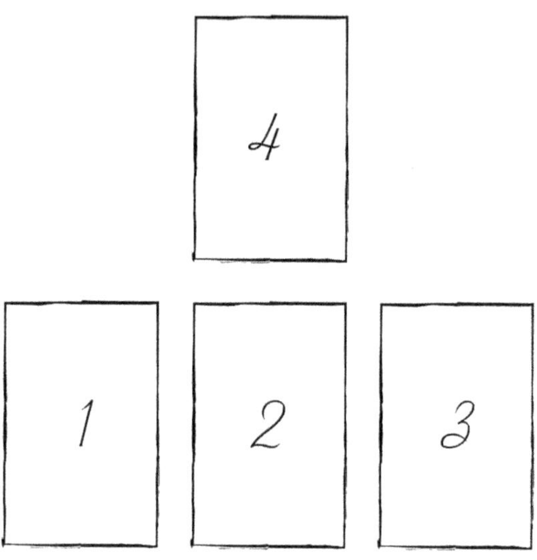

Part 2 – my weaknesses

1. Which of my weaknesses am I the most comfortable with?

2. Which of my weaknesses am I the least comfortable with?

3. Which of my weaknesses am I forgetting about?

4. What about these weaknesses might trip me up here?

Part 3 – turning my weaknesses into strengths

1. For each of the three weaknesses that came up in the previous spread, draw a card, asking, 'What potential strength is hidden underneath this weakness?'

2. For each card drawn, draw another, asking, 'How do I bring out this potential strength and make it work for me?'

6

THE PLAN OF ATTACK

Whether you're starting a new business venture, collaboration, or project, this spread will provide you with the necessary clarity to start your new endeavour with the energy and mindset you need to be successful.

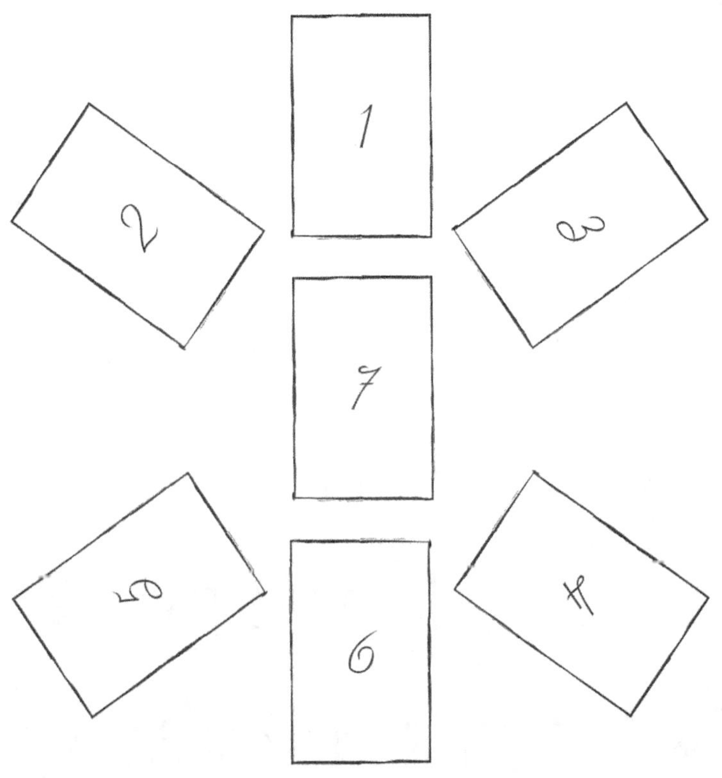

1. What energy surrounds this endeavour?

2. How can I clear or utilise this energy?

3. What energy do I need to bring to this endeavour?

4. What known aspects do I need to look out for?

5. What unknown aspects do I need to look out for?

6. What do I need to remember about myself right now?

7. What do I need to remember about this endeavour?

7

AM I READY TO JUMP?

No matter what you're getting ready for – an entirely new business, a new business avenue, a new partnership or collaboration, or a new project – use this spread to set yourself up for a successful leap.

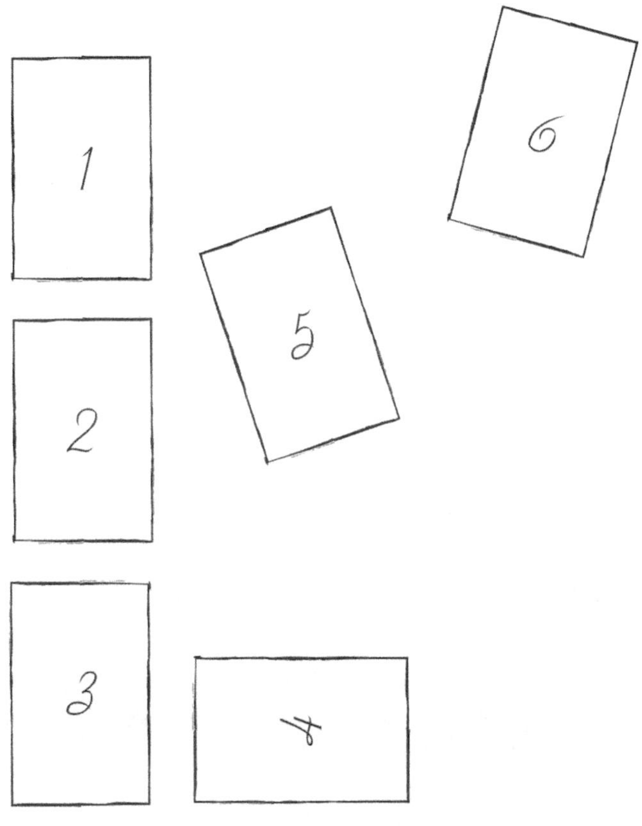

1. Why haven't I taken the leap yet?

2. What do I have to consider before taking this leap?

3. What kind of safety net do I need to create before jumping?

4. How do I set up this safety net?

5. How will I know when I'm ready to jump?

6. General advice about the leap I'm about to take.

Succeed

Now that you've set yourself up for success, the card spreads included in this section will help you discard whatever might be limiting you and align yourself and your purpose with what's needed in the world so success can flow your way freely.

8

MY SUCCESS IS INEVITABLE

While this spread was specifically created with new, upcoming projects in mind, it can also be used to ask about other business undertakings, such as collaborations or entire new businesses. Simply swap the word 'project' for 'collaboration' or 'business' and sling those cards.

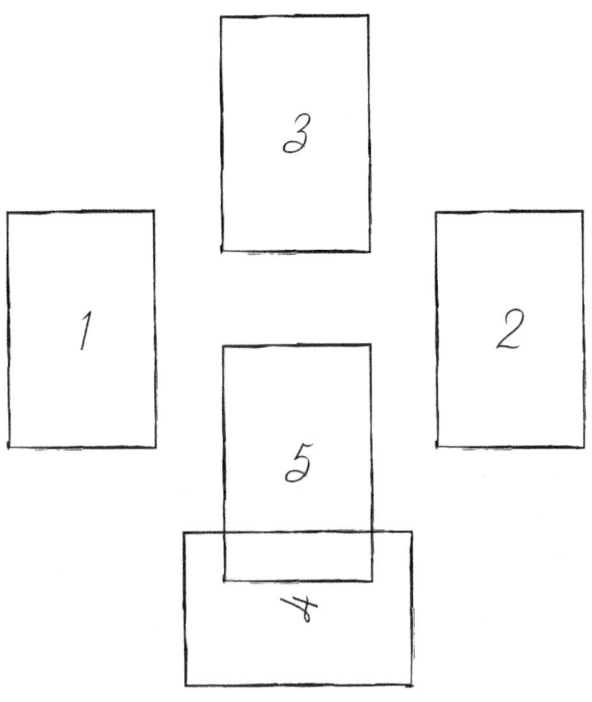

1. What am I expecting from this project?

2. What can I expect from this project?

3. How can I best shift or align my expectations?

4. Where am I potentially blocking my chances of success?

5. How do I clear these potential blocks and guarantee my success?

9

WHAT GOES AROUND COMES AROUND

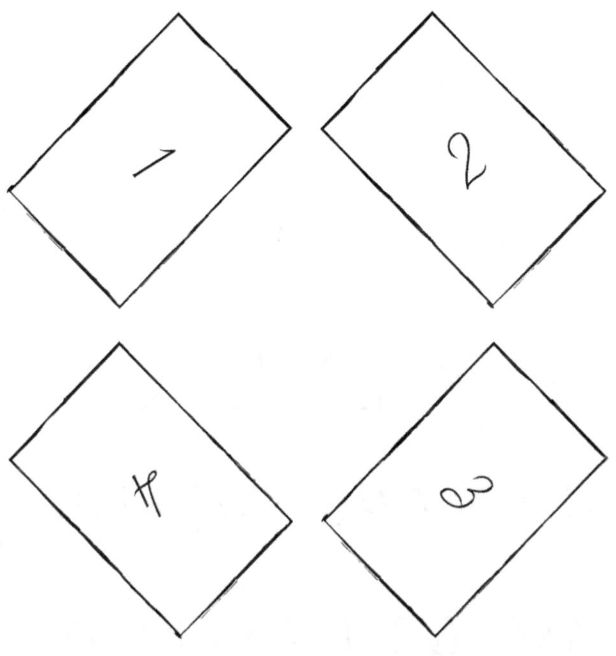

1. What do I have to offer to the world right now?

2. How do I allow that energy to flow outwards freely?

3. How might this energy be returned to me?

4. How do I open myself up to receiving that energy

back fully?

10

MY ENERGY FLOWS WHERE MY ATTENTION GOES

If you know exactly what you're trying to manifest, you can pick a signifier card and put it in place of Question 1. A signifier card is a card that's intentionally chosen before a deck is shuffled and the rest of a spread is laid.

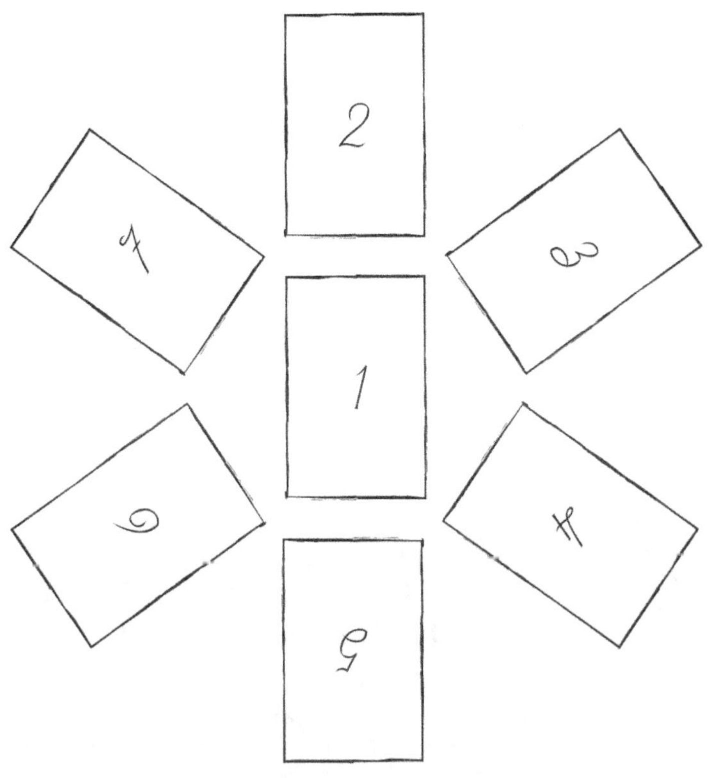

1. What am I trying to manifest?

2. Why do I want to manifest this?

3. What do I need to know about manifesting this?

4. How am I already manifesting this?

5. How am I currently blocking this from becoming fully manifested?

6. How do I dissolve this block?

7. What can I do right now to bring what I want to manifest a step closer to being actualised?

11
STEPPING INTO THE LIGHT

1. Where am I keeping myself invisible?

2. How I am keeping myself invisible?

3. Why am I keeping myself invisible?

4. Why do I want to be more visible?

5. How will better visibility benefit me?

6. How will my improved visibility benefit others?

7. How do I begin to step into the light?

8. How can I anticipate the fears wanting to drag me

back into the shadows?

12
MY MONEY STORY

What am I telling myself about money?

If you experience any struggles around money, this three-part spread will help you understand your money story and where it's coming from.

If you do all three parts of this spread, please remember to write down the results of your draw and return all cards to the deck after each part to shuffle them anew.

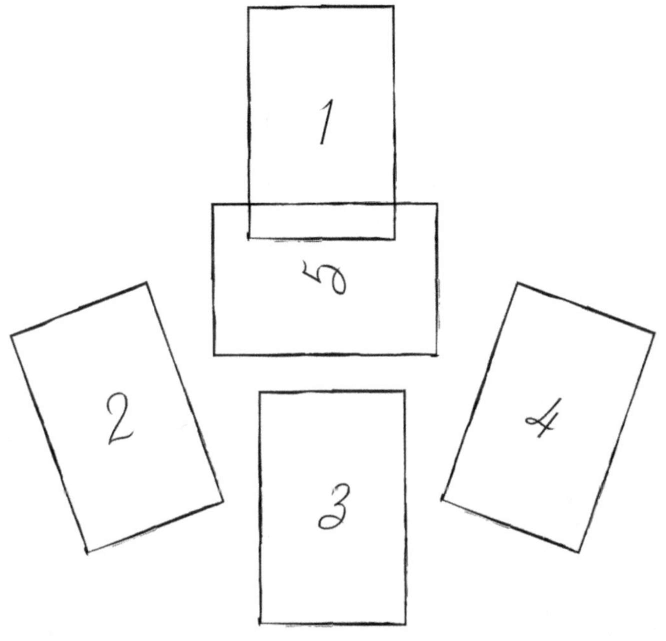

Part 1 – the past

1. What do I tell myself about where I used to be money-wise?

2. Why am I telling this story to myself?

3. Where does this story come from?

4. Why do I keep repeating this particular story?

5. How is this story blocking me in the here and now?

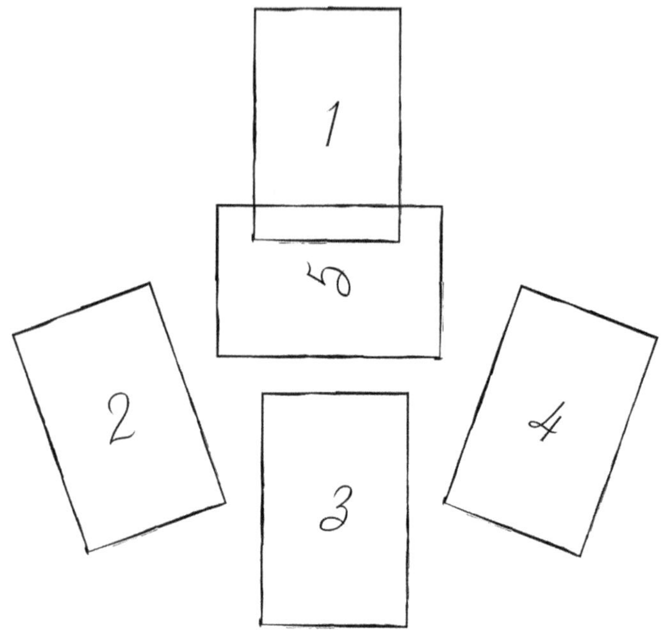

Part 2 – the present

1. What do I tell myself about where I am now money-wise?

2. Why am I telling this story to myself?

3. Where does this story come from?

4. Why do I keep repeating this particular story?

5. How is this story blocking me in the here and now?

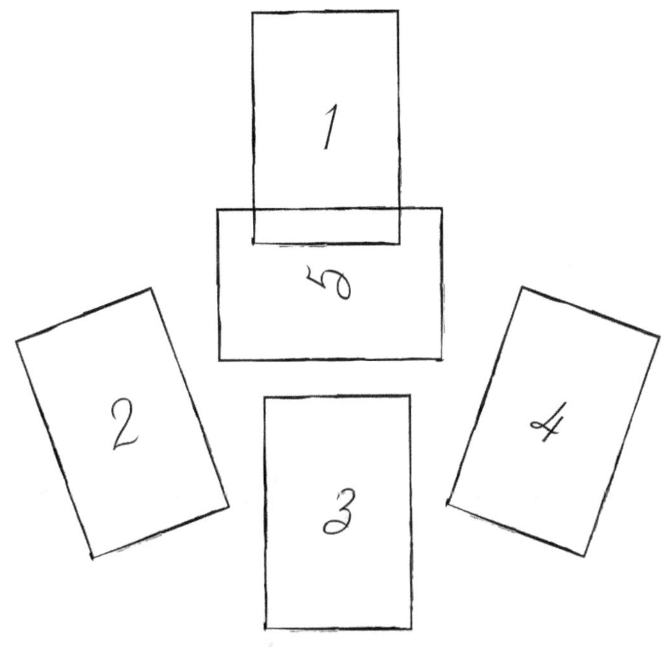

Part 3 – the future

1. What do I tell myself about where I will be money-wise?

2. Why am I telling this story to myself?

3. Where does this story come from?

4. Why do I keep repeating this particular story?

5. How is this story blocking me in the here and now?

13

MY MONEY STORY

How do I change it?

During the previous spread, you figured out the different money stories you are telling yourself, where they came from, and how they are affecting you and your entrepreneurial endeavours today. This spread will help you rewrite your money story in a way that best fits your current and future self.

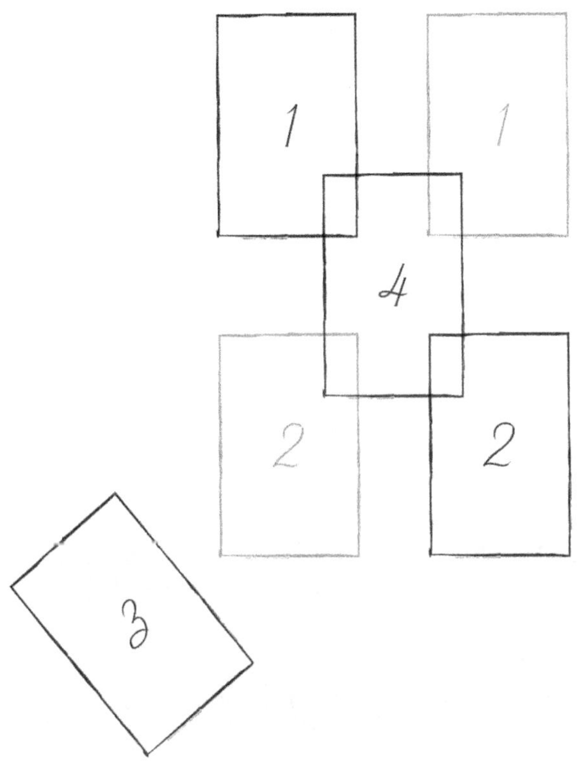

1. What money story best aligns with my current reality?

(Draw up to two cards.)

2. What money story best aligns with where I'm headed in the future?

(Draw up to two cards.)

3. How do I let go of my old money stories?

4. How do I create space for my new money stories to fully take root?

14
MIND THE GAP

Aligning myself with my clients' needs

Although I used the word 'client' in this spread, this can mean anything, depending on what kind of business you run. Feel free to swap the term for something like 'audience', 'customer', or 'reader'.

While interpreting your results, remember that this is not a spread about your ideal client. As such, keep an open mind: the spread could be trying to tell you that you've been directing your attention to the wrong audience.

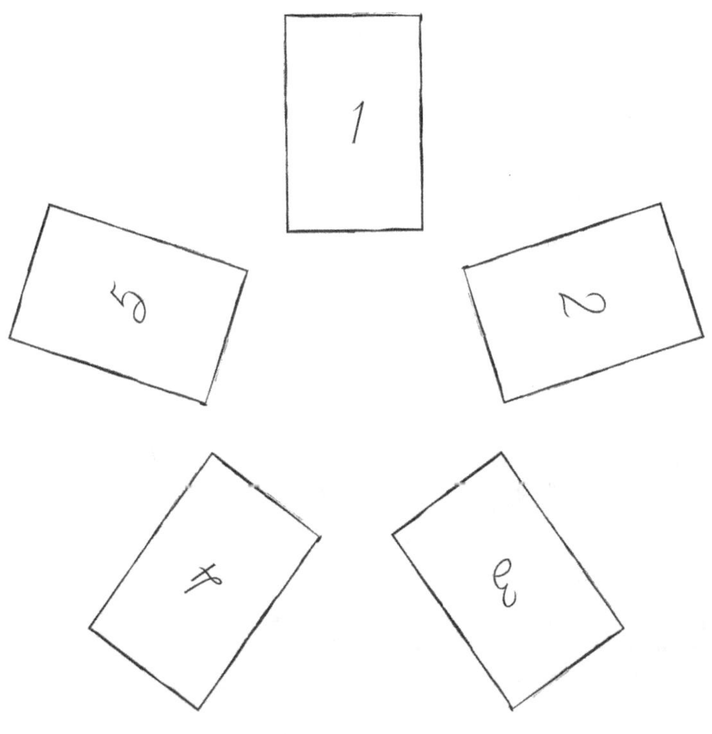

1. How am I meeting my clients' needs?

2. Where aren't I meeting their needs?

3. What is keeping me from meeting these particular needs?

4. How can I best bridge this gap?

5. General advice about meeting my clients' needs.

Sustain

If you're in this for the long run, the following card spreads will
help you make your business sustainable by showing you how
best to take care of yourself and your (business) needs.

15

I HONOUR MY BOUNDARIES

and don't let myself cross them

As someone who's struggled with workaholism for most of her adult life, I'm no stranger to taking on too much. If you're anything like me – that is, prone to saying 'Yes' more often than is good for you – you should definitely try this spread. If this struggle extends to your personal life, this spread can absolutely be used to address those situations as well.

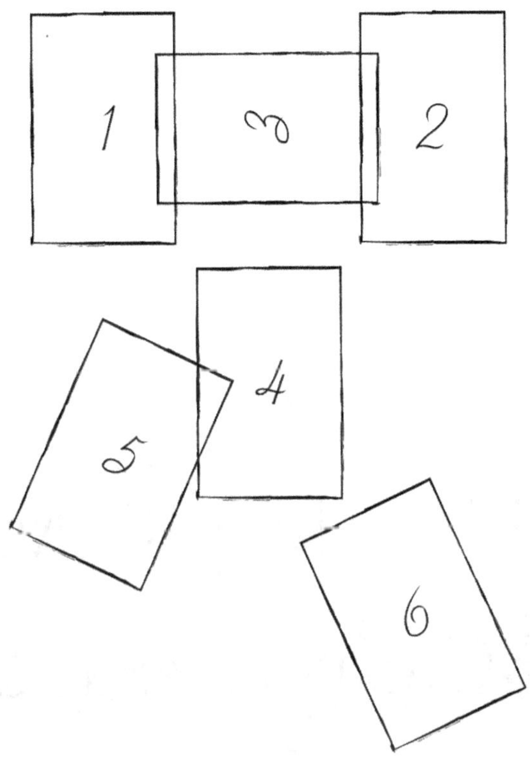

1. Where have I taken on too much?

2. Why have I taken on too much here?

3. What happens if I continue the way things are going?

4. What happens if I take a step back now?

5. How can I best take that step back?

6. How can I keep myself from crossing my own boundaries

in the future?

16

I HONOUR MY BOUNDARIES

and don't let others cross them

If you have a client (or customer, reader, staff member, business partner, etc.) who keeps crossing your boundaries, this spread will help you reset them and take back your personal power. You can also use this spread in a non-business context – for example, with a loved one, a neighbour, or whoever else might be crossing your boundaries right now.

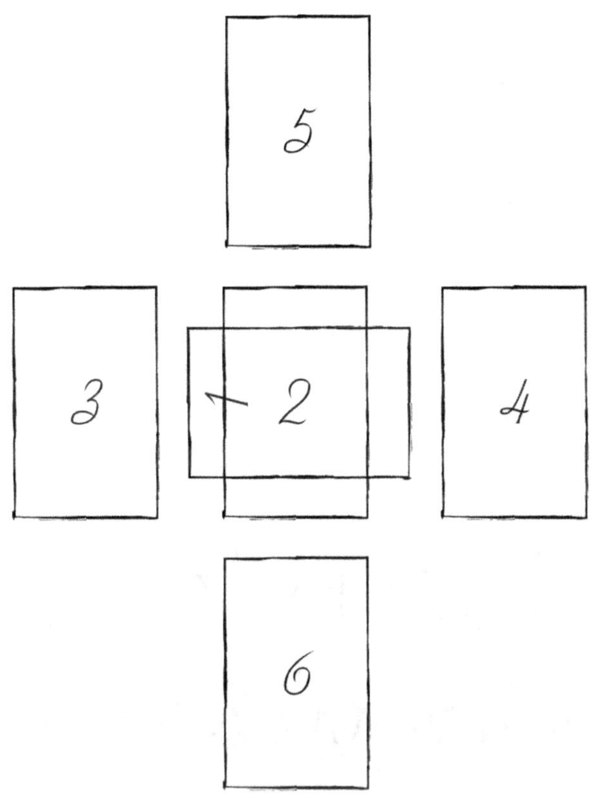

1. Why is this client crossing my boundaries?

2. What part do I play in this situation?

3. How can I best make my boundaries clear(er) to them?

4. What do I do when the situation doesn't change for the better?

5. How do I make my boundaries clear – to this or other clients –

in the future?

6. General advice about this situation.

17
SUPPLY AND DEMAND

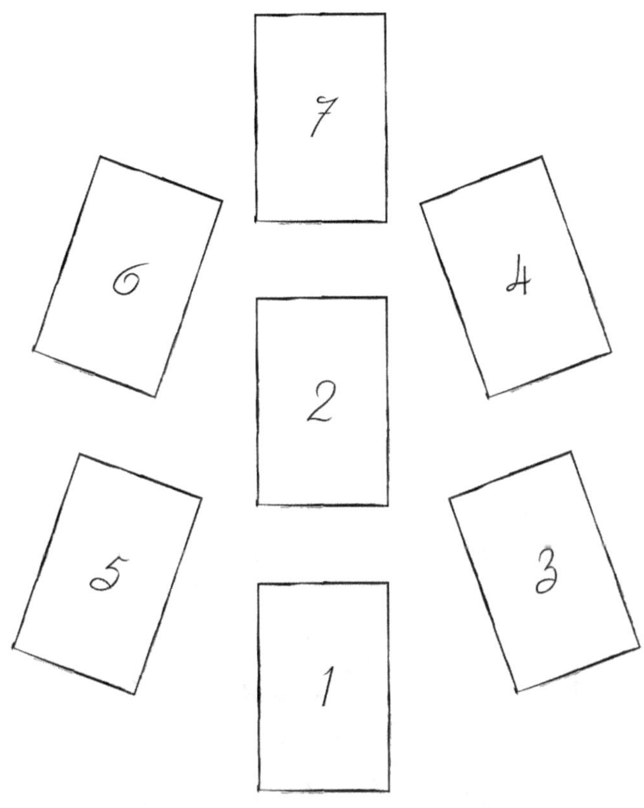

1. What does the world need right now?

2. What can I offer the world right now?

3. Where do the world's needs align with what I can supply?

4. How can I best meet these needs?

5. Where don't the world's needs align with what I can supply?

6. How do I fully accept and move on from this?

7. What shouldn't I forget about what I have to offer?

18

I AM WORTH MY WEIGHT IN GOLD

Asking for what you're worth is hard. In fact, it might be the hardest thing you ever do. This spread will help you determine where your current rates are at and whether it's time to change them.

If you're still getting started and aren't charging anyone anything yet, take the rates you're thinking of asking and use this spread to put them to the test.

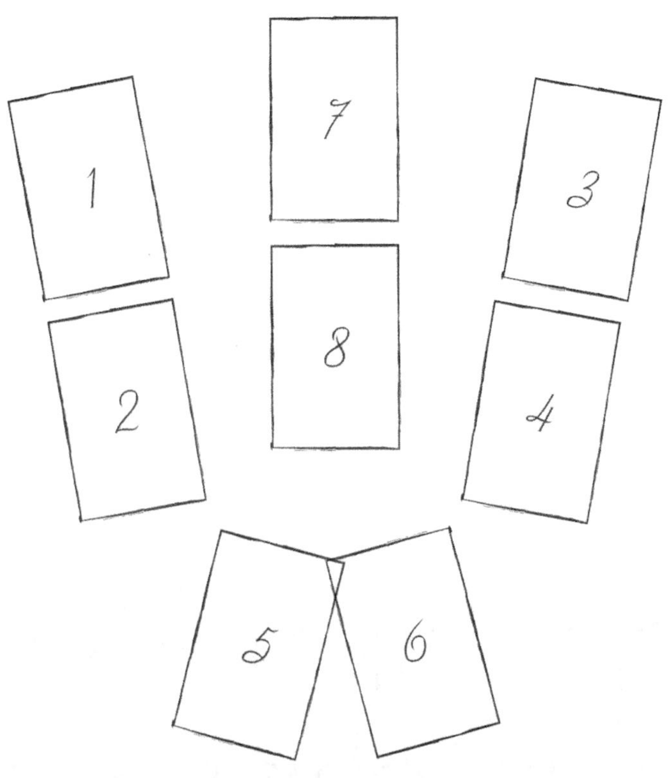

1. Why am I charging my current rates?

2. What do I need to know about my current rates?

3. How am I currently feeling about my worth?

4. What do I need to know about my worth?

5. How aligned are my current rates with what I'm worth?

6. How do I (better) align my rates with what I'm worth?

7. How can I best explain any changes in what I'm charging to my audience?

8. General advice on asking for what I'm worth.

19

STRAIGHTENING PRIORITIES

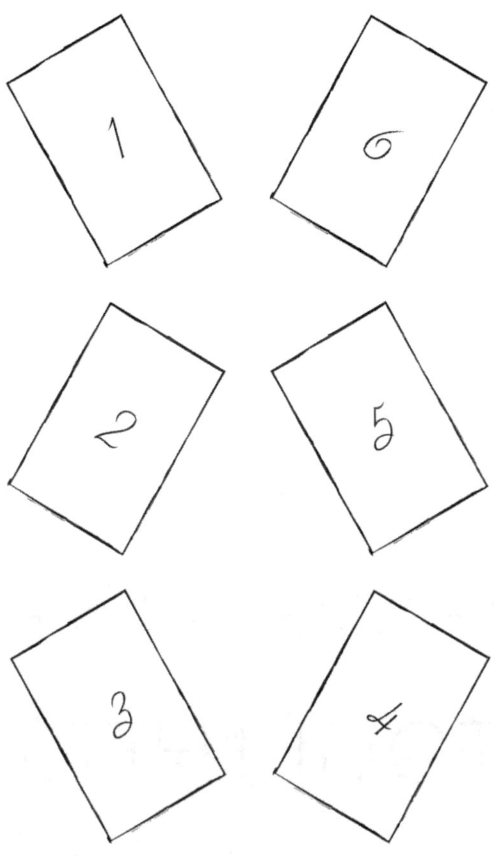

1. Why am I struggling to prioritise?

2. What do I want to prioritise right now?

3. What should I be prioritising right now?

4. Why should I prioritise this?

5. What can I do to keep this a priority for as long as I need to?

6. General advice about keeping my priorities straight.

ARE WE IN THIS TOGETHER?

Are you working with someone or something and you just can't help but feel they're not putting in the same amount of time and effort? If yes, this spread will help you shine some light on the situation and what's going on exactly.

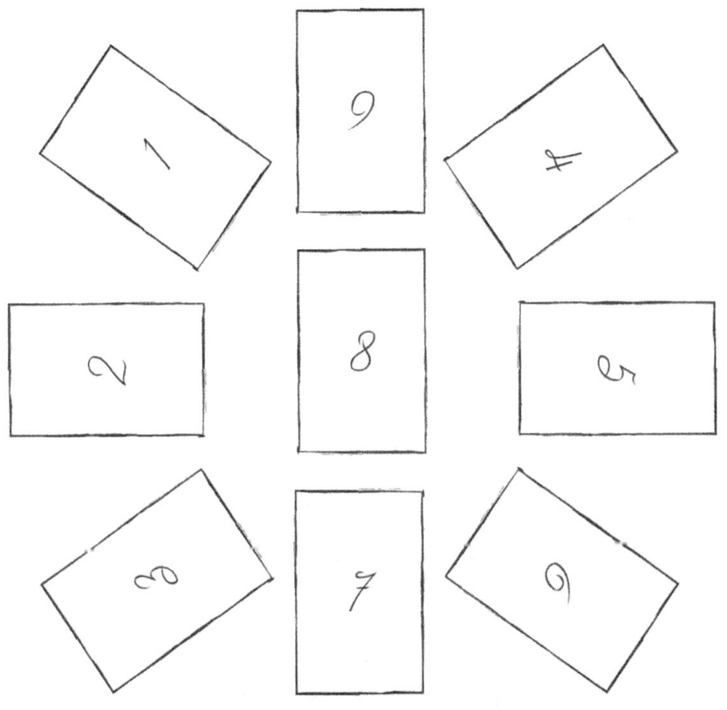

1. What have I been giving to this collaboration?

2. What have I been getting from this collaboration?

3. What do I need to know about my efforts?

4. What have my collaborators been giving to this collaboration?

5. What have my collaborators been getting from this collaboration?

6. What do I need to know about their efforts?

7. Why do I feel the balance is off?

8. What can I do to restore a sense of balance?

9. General advice about this collaboration.

21

CHECKING IN AND TUNING UP

This four-part spread allows you to check in with and tune up the four human bodies: the physical, the emotional, the mental, and the spiritual. You can either do all four spreads in one sitting or pick the body you want to check in on in this moment.

If you do all three parts of this spread, please remember to write down the results of your draw and return all cards to the deck after each part to shuffle them anew.

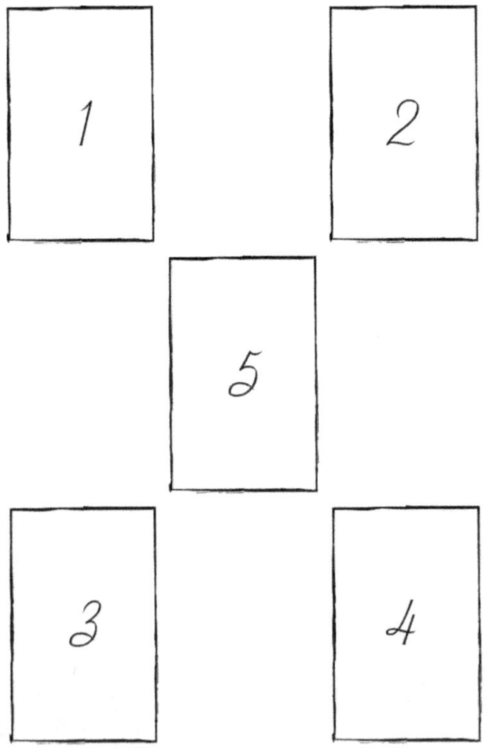

Part 1 – the physical body

1. How am I doing physically?

2. How did I end up here?

3. How can I best take care of myself physically right now?

4. How can I best take care of myself physically in the long run?

5. General advice on taking care of my physical body.

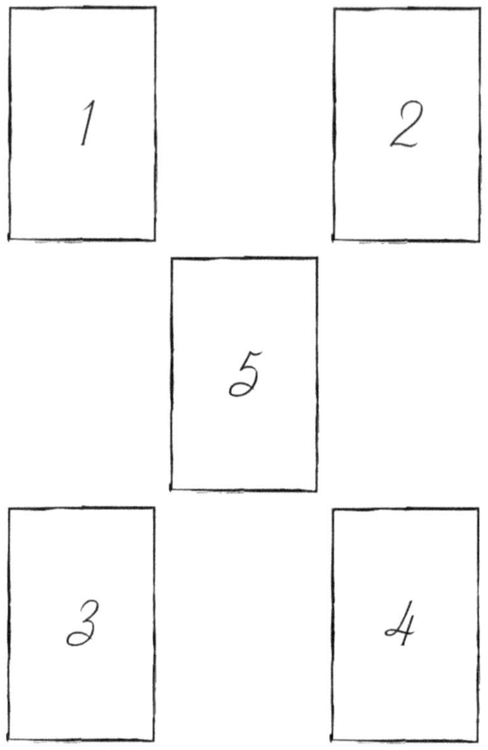

Part 2 – the emotional body

1. How am I doing emotionally?

2. How did I end up here?

3. How can I best take care of myself emotionally right now?

4. How can I best take care of myself emotionally in the long run?

5. General advice on taking care of my emotional body.

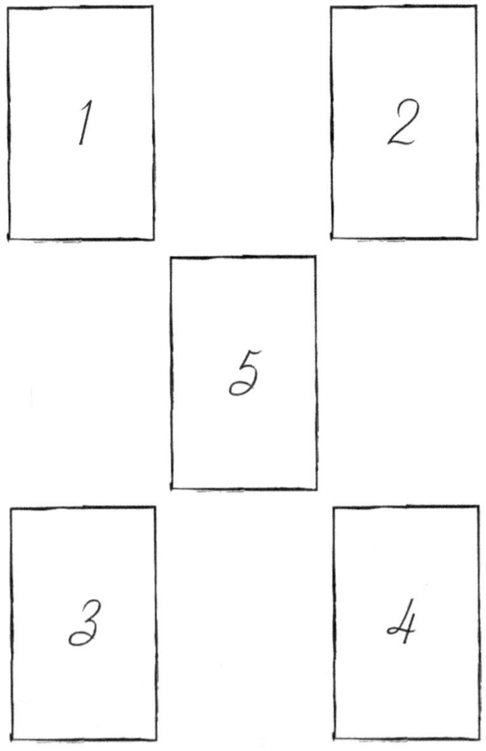

Part 3 – the mental body

1. How am I doing mentally?

2. How did I end up here?

3. How can I best take care of myself mentally right now?

4. How can I best take care of myself mentally in the long run?

5. General advice on taking care of my mental body.

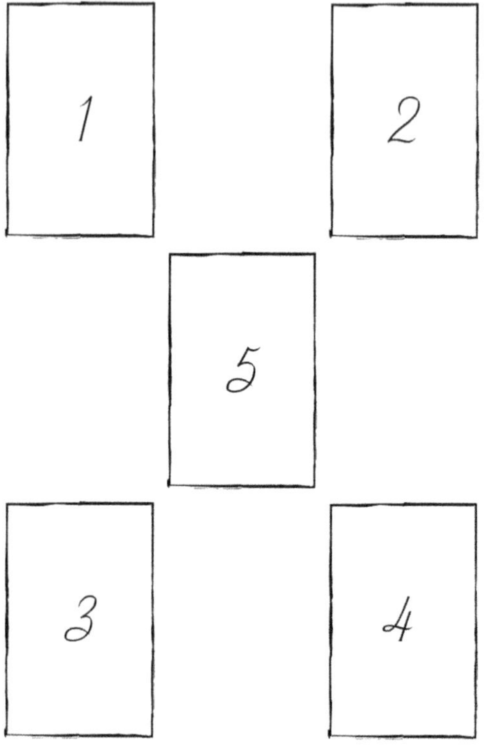

Part 4 – the spiritual body

1. How am I doing spiritually?

2. How did I end up here?

3. How can I best take care of myself spiritually right now?

4. How can I best take care of myself spiritually in the long run?

5. General advice on taking care of my spiritual body.

(be)
Sovereign

Remaining sovereign in an overly opiniated world is a form of art. The spreads in this section will help you choose yourself and stand in your own power so you can carve your own path and stay true to your sovereign self.

22

EVERYONE ELSE IS DOING IT

but what if I don't want to?

Peer pressure. No matter what line of business you're in, you will come across those who are doing the same or something similar as you. And that is great because we all need people who understand what we're doing, where we're coming from, and what we're dealing with.

However, being surrounded by like-doing people doesn't mean they're also like-minded and that their way of doing things aligns with us. If that's something you're struggling with right now, this spread will help you figure out what course of action is best for you.

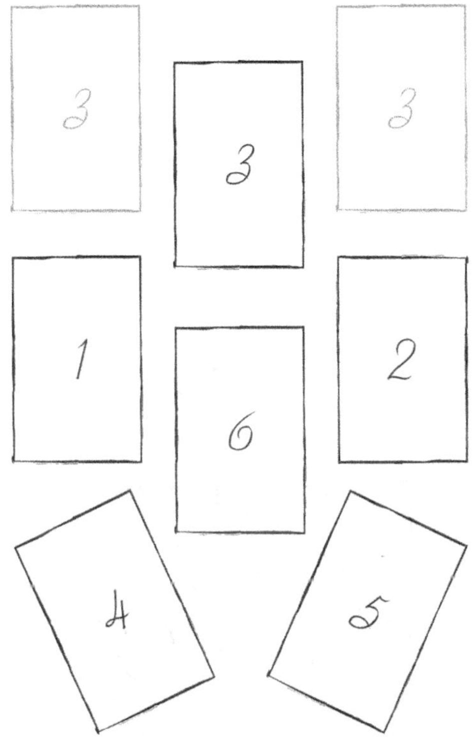

1. Why is everyone doing X?

2. Why do I feel I have to do things the same way?

3. What other options are available to me?

(Draw up to three cards.)

4. What is the most likely outcome if I do it the way others are doing it?

5. What is the most likely outcome if I do things in a way that's more

aligned with me?

6. General advice on staying true to myself while my peers are doing

things their way.

23
TO HEED OR NOT TO HEED

this piece of advice

It can be hard to distinguish good advice from bad advice, especially when you're not 100% sure you know what you're doing – and if that's the case, welcome to the club! None of us have a clue, not really.

This spread will help you figure out whether a particular piece of advice is in any way aligned with you or whether it's best to disregard it and do something else instead.

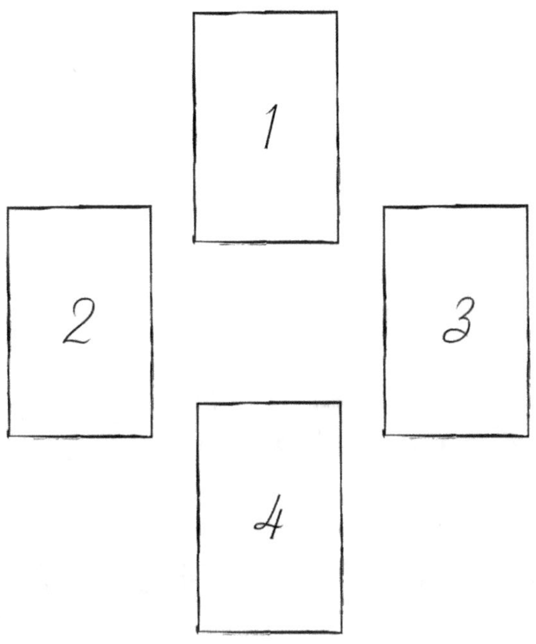

1. Why have I been given this piece of advice?

2. Why am I inclined to consider this piece of advice

for myself?

3. Why doesn't this piece of advice resonate with me?

4. What advice should I be following?

24

HOW DO I SAY 'NO' TO THIS?

I initially created this spread with entrepreneurship on my mind, intending it to be used for dealing with projects, clients, staff members, and so on. However, it quickly dawned on me that this spread can be used for anything or anyone we feel inclined to say 'No' to.

As someone who struggles with saying 'No' herself, I keep this spread close at all times.

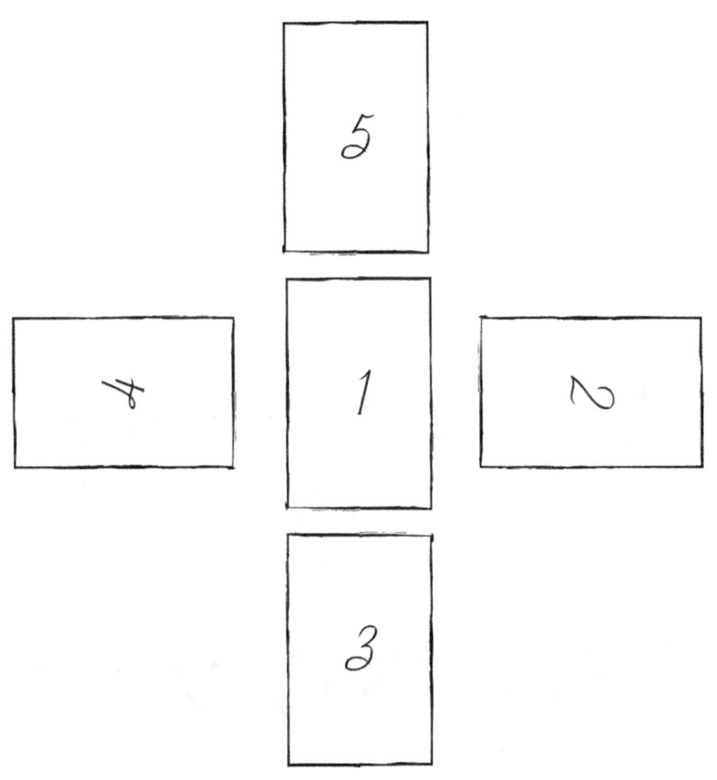

1. Why do I want to say 'No' to this?

2. Why am I struggling to simply say 'No'?

3. What's the most likely outcome if I don't say 'No'?

4. What's the most likely outcome if I do say 'No'?

5. How do I say 'No' to this?

25

SELLING MYSELF WITHOUT SELLING MY SOUL

If you're in business, there's no way out of it: you will have to market yourself, or what you're offering at the very least. Many entrepreneurs struggle with this part of the business, but remember: there's nothing wrong with letting people know exactly what you have to offer them. In fact, it's the only way to get an audience and find your ideal client. If the word 'marketing' makes you itch in all the wrong ways, give this spread a go and see what it says.

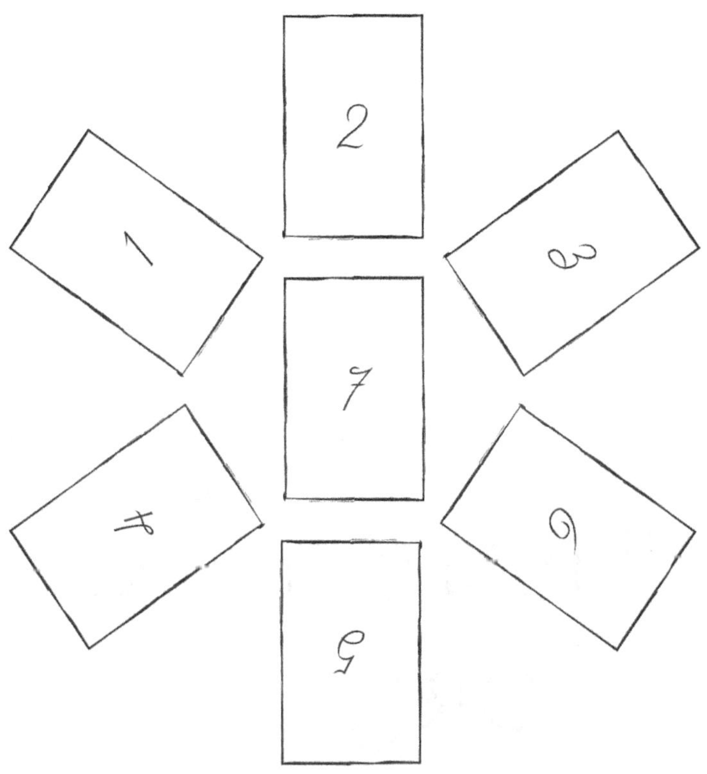

1. What kind of marketing strategy is the most aligned with me?

2. Why is this kind of marketing strategy the most aligned with me?

3. How do I say 'Yes' to this kind of strategy?

4. What kind of marketing strategy is the least aligned with me?

5. Why is this kind of marketing strategy the least aligned with me?

6. How do I say 'No' to this kind of strategy?

7. General advice on keeping my marketing strategy true to myself.

26

HEAD, HEART, OR GUT?

Which do I go with?

If you're feeling pulled in multiple directions about a situation, this three-part spread will help you figure out which part of you – your head, heart, or gut – is trying to tell you what, and which of the three to listen to.

If you do all three parts of this spread, please remember to write down the results of your draw and return all cards to the deck after each part to shuffle them anew.

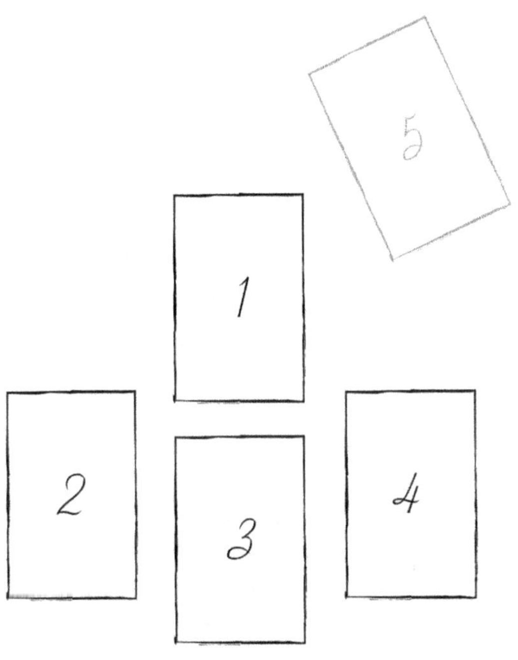

Part 1 – head

1. How does my head perceive this situation?

2. Why does my head perceive this situation as such?

3. What do I need to remember about how my head tends to

perceive things?

4. What'll happen if I follow my head here?

5. General advice about the decision ahead.

(If you're only drawing cards for Part 1, then answer this question

now. If, however, you're drawing cards for Parts 1–3, skip this

question and ask it after drawing cards for Part 3.)

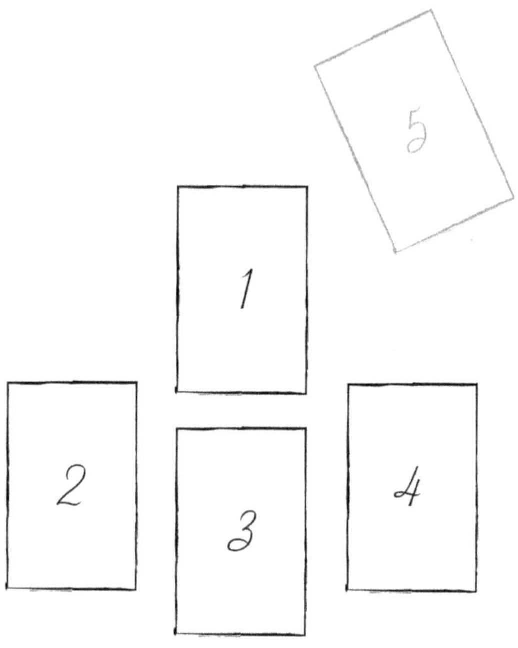

Part 2 – heart

1. How does my heart feel about this situation?

2. Why does my heart feel this way about this situation?

3. What do I need to remember about how my heart tends to
feel about things?

4. What'll happen if I follow my heart here?

5. General advice about the decision ahead.

(If you're only drawing cards for Part 2, then answer this

question now. If, however, you're drawing cards for Parts 1–3,

skip this question and ask it after drawing cards for Part 3.)

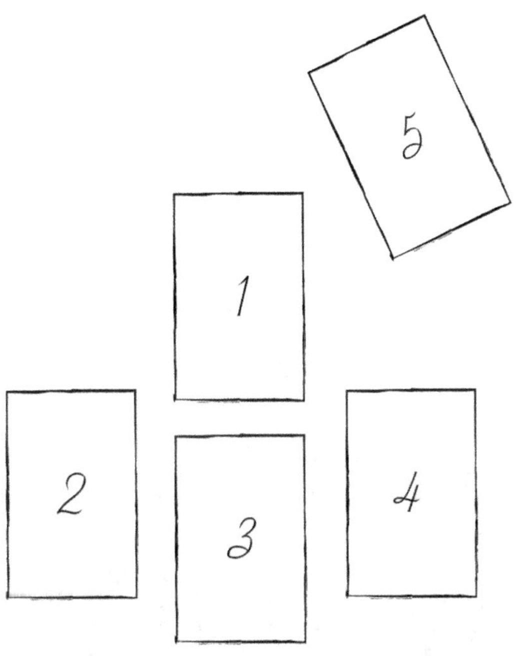

Part 3 – gut

1. How does my gut intuit this situation?

2. Why does my gut intuit this situation as such?

3. What do I need to remember about how my gut tends

to intuit things?

4. What'll happen if I follow my gut here?

5. General advice about the decision ahead.

27

WHAT'S WRONG WITH THIS PICTURE?

Is this the right client for me?

Ever have that feeling that something isn't quite right when you're talking with a potential new client? This spread will help you figure out whether your unease is warranted and whether or not to do business with this client.

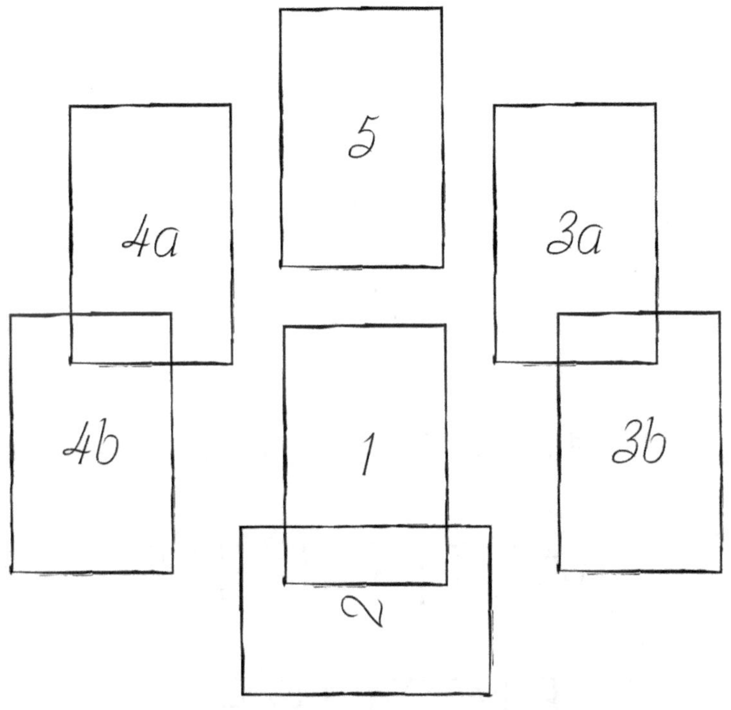

1. What do I know about this client?

2. What don't I know about this client?

3. How could this client benefit me and my company now (a)

and in the future (b)?

4. How could this client hurt me and my company now (a)

and in the future (b)?

5. What must I remember about myself and my company

before I make a decision about this client?

28

WHAT'S WRONG WITH THIS PICTURE?

Is this the right project for me?

This is the perfect spread to use when something keeps feeling off about a project and you just can't put your finger on it. Of course, you can use the same spread for investments, collaborations, or anything that doesn't feel quite right, no matter how hard you've been trying to convince yourself otherwise.

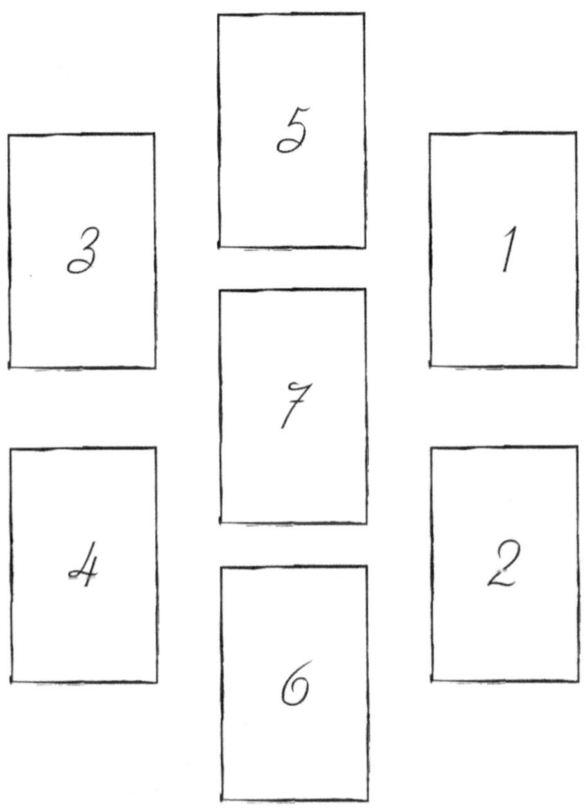

1. What do I know about this project?

2. What don't I know about this project?

3. How is this project aligned with me right now?

4. How isn't this project aligned with me right now?

5. What do I stand to gain?

6. What do I stand to lose?

7. General advice about this project.

Switch

Whether or not you've invited certain changes into your business (Hello, Tower card!), the spreads in this section will help you figure out what needs to change, how to go about it, and what's next for you.

29
THE WIND OF CHANGE

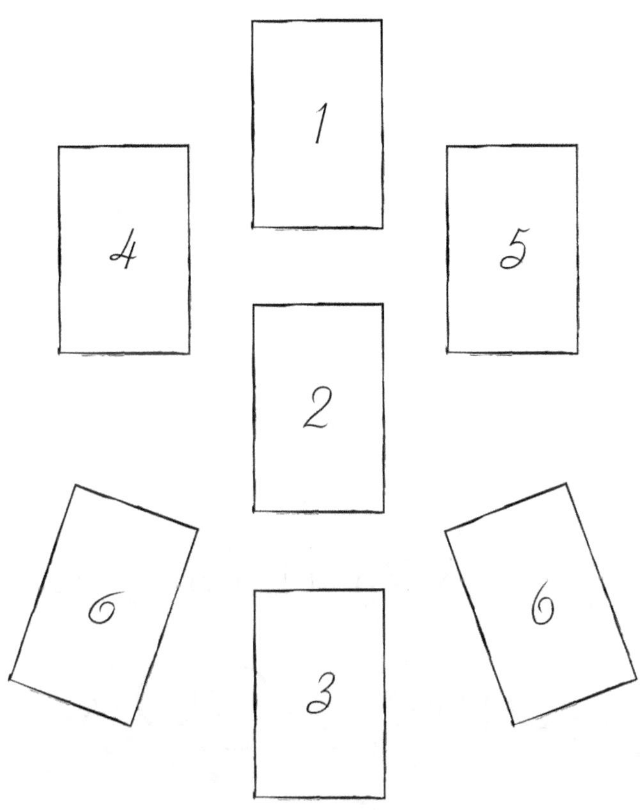

1. Where am I right now?

2. What kind of change have I been craving?

3. Why have I been craving this change?

4. What needs to go?

5. What must stay?

6. General advice on the desired change.

(Draw two cards.)

30

WHEN ONE DOOR CLOSES...

We all know what it feels like when that one door, that door we've been aiming for, slams shut in our face. We also all know that a new door is supposed to open when that happens, but it isn't always easy to navigate new opportunities when we've just lost something we (thought we) wanted. This spread will help you find your bearings.

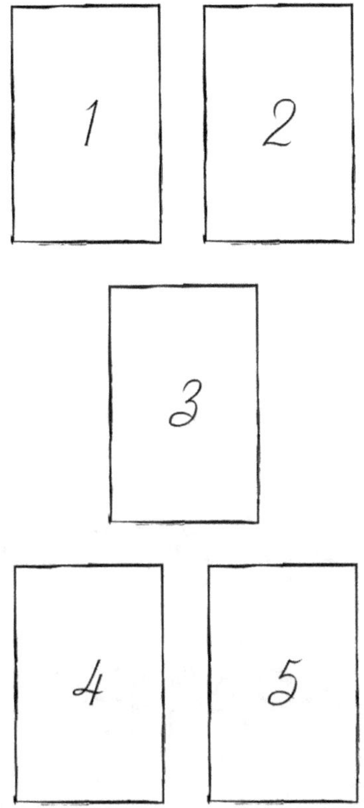

1. Why did this door close on me?

2. How can I best process this loss?

3. What door opened in the meantime?

4. Why did this new door open for me?

5. How do I prepare myself for stepping through this new door?

31

THE RIGHT PATH

Whether you find yourself at a crossroads or are simply contemplating changing directions, this spread will help you get clear on what your options are and which path is currently right for you.

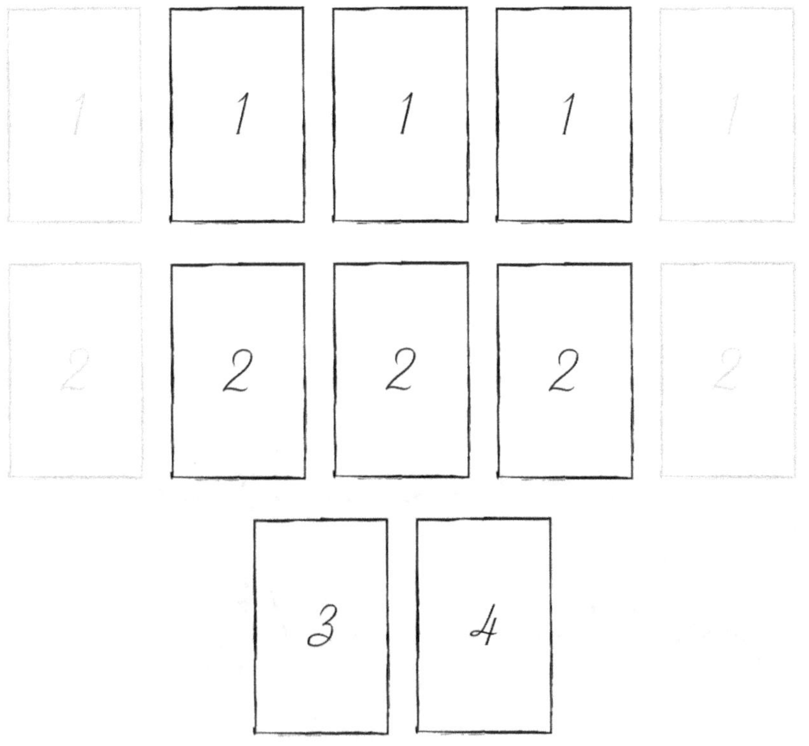

1. Which paths are available to me right now?

(Draw three to five cards.)

2. What do I need to know about each of these paths?

(Draw a card for each card drawn in answer to Question 1.)

3. How do I pick the path that's best for me right now?

4. General advice about what's currently the best path for me.

32

CHOOSING LOVE OVER FEAR

A signifier card is a card that's intentionally chosen before a deck is shuffled and the rest of a spread is laid. If you aren't 100% sure about your answer to Question 1, don't worry about picking a signifier: just shuffle your cards and let them answer for you.

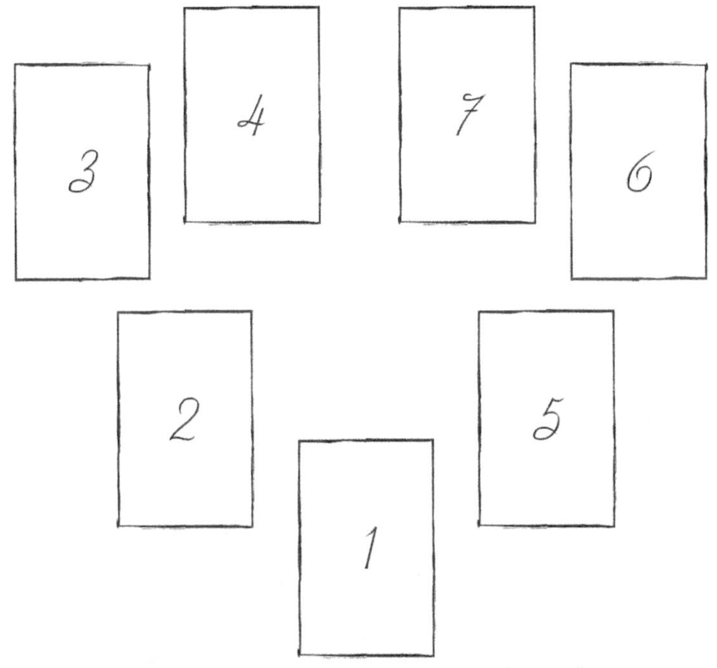

1. Where have I chosen fear over love in my business?

(If you already know the answer to this, pick or pull a signifier card to

represent this area.)

2. Why did I choose fear over love here?

3. Where did this fear come from?

4. How can I best challenge this fear?

5. What does choosing love over fear look like for me in this situation?

6. What would be different now if I had chosen love over fear instead?

7. How can I choose love over fear from now on?

33

TIME TO
DELEGATE?

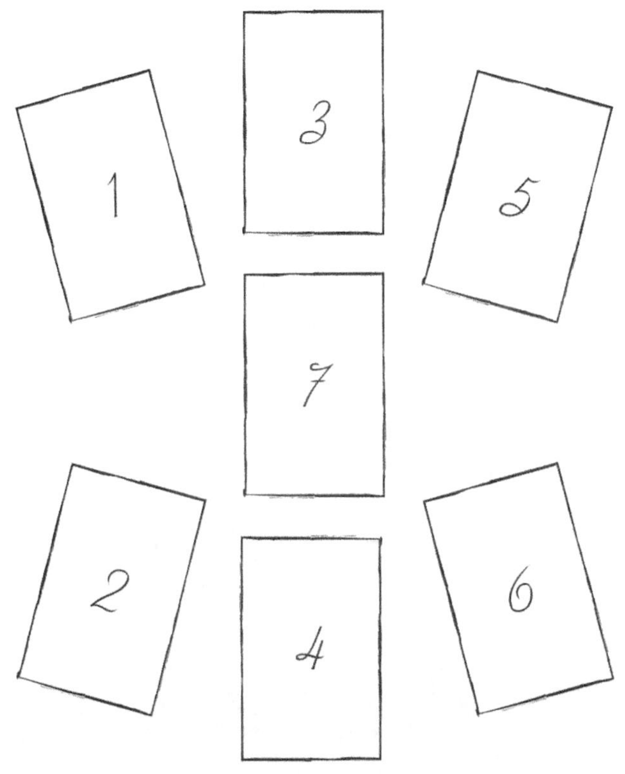

1. What should I be doing myself?

2. Why should I be doing this myself?

3. What should I delegate right away?

4. Why should I delegate this right away?

5. What should I be delegating in the future?

6. Why should I be delegating this in the future?

7. How will I know it's time to start delegating more?

Stretch

As entrepreneurs, there are a myriad of ways in which you can expand and grow and a myriad of reasons why you might want or need to. The spreads in this section will help you figure out what you might want or need to expand, why you feel like spreading your wings, and what you need to know about this growth.

34

IS IT TIME TO EXPAND?

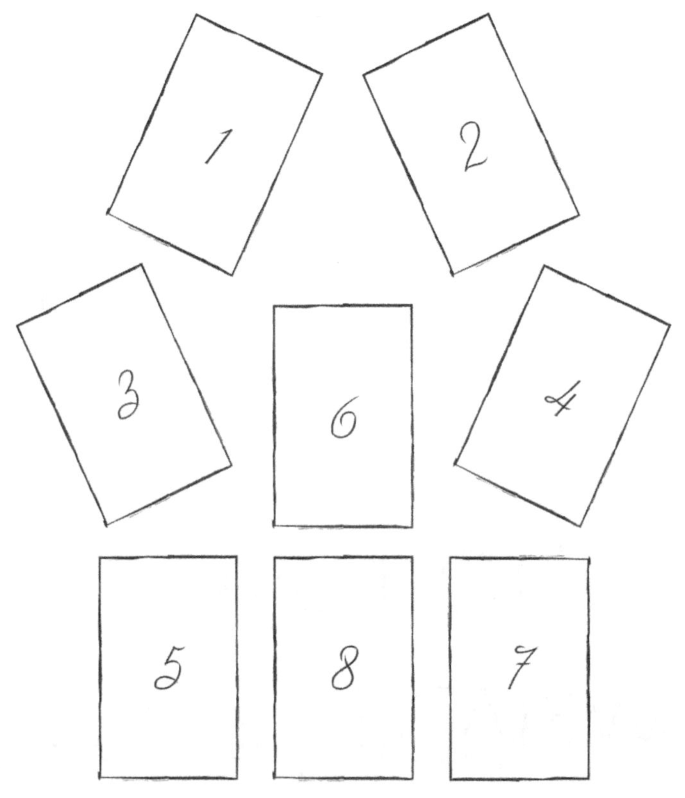

1. Why do I feel like expanding?

2. Why isn't what I have now enough for me?

3. What do I want more of?

4. Why do I want more of that?

5. In which direction would I have to expand to receive more of that?

6. How should I go about this expansion?

7. What is the first step I can take to realise this?

8. General advice on expanding in this direction.

35

DO I HAVE WHAT IT TAKES

to level up?

1. What does 'leveling up' mean to me?

2. What could 'leveling up' look like for me?

3. How do I want to level up?

4. What do I know about this desire to level up?
(Draw up to two cards.)

5. What don't I know about this desire to level up?
(Draw up to two cards.)

6. How will I know whether I'm ready to level up?

7. How will I know when to level up?

8. General advice on taking things to the next level.

36

IS THIS BEYOND ME?

You want to – really, really want to – yet part of you isn't all that convinced you're ready to tackle project X, work with client Y, or dive into opportunity Z. This spread will help you shush your imposter syndrome so you can figure out for yourself whether or not you've truly got this.

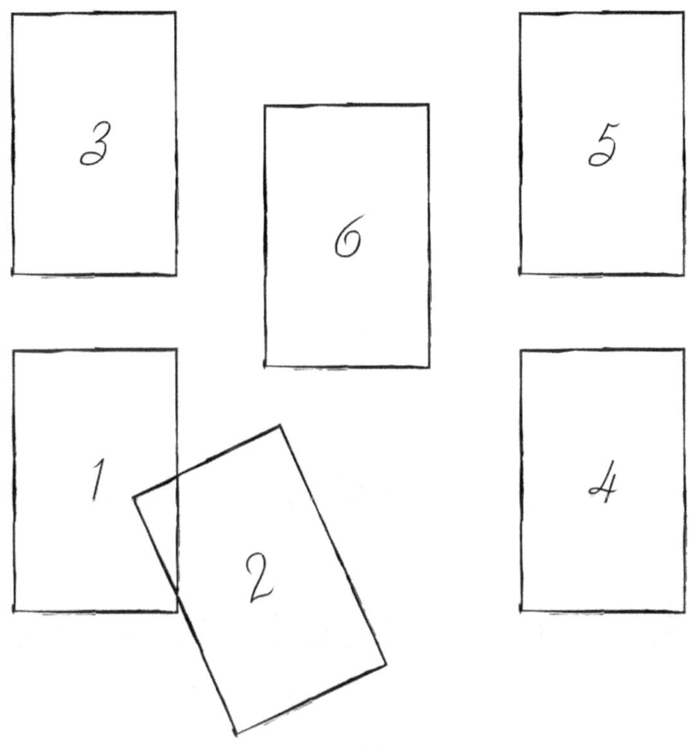

1. What makes me want to take this on?

2. Why do I doubt my ability to handle this?

3. Which existing skills can I rely on?

4. Which skills might I need to improve?

5. Where can I turn for help with this?

6. What must I remember about myself here?

37

NO ENTREPRENEUR IS AN ISLAND

To succeed, community is vital. Whether or not we can make it on our own, everyone thrives better with the right kind of people providing the right kind of support. If you've been feeling somewhat isolated lately, this spread will guide you towards the people you need to surround yourself with right now.

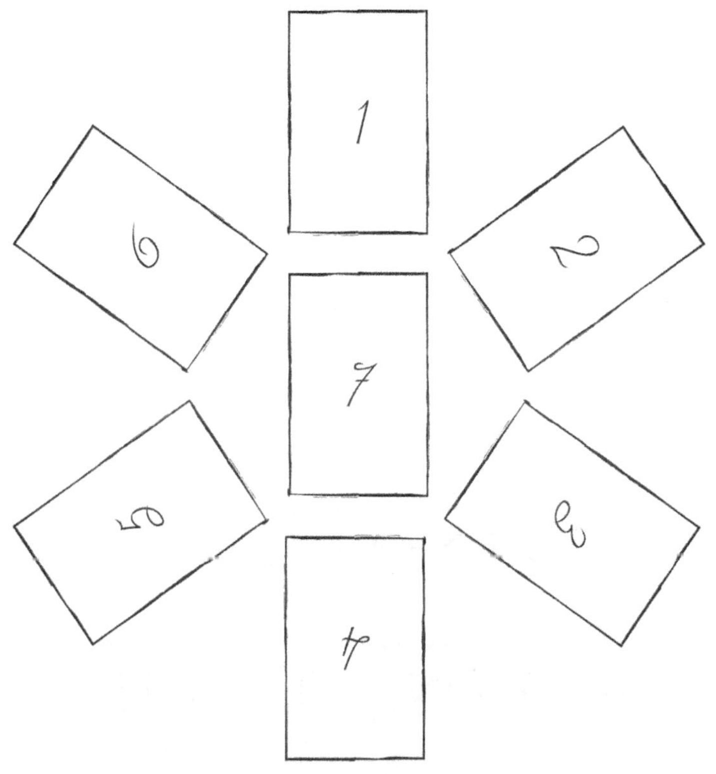

1. What kind of people do I need in my life right now?

2. Why do I need to connect to these people?

3. Where will I find these people?

4. How will I recognise them?

5. What can they give me that I can't give myself right now?

6. What will I be able to give to them that they can't give themselves

right now?

7. General advice on connecting with the right kind of people for me.

38

IS THIS WORTH THE INVESTMENT?

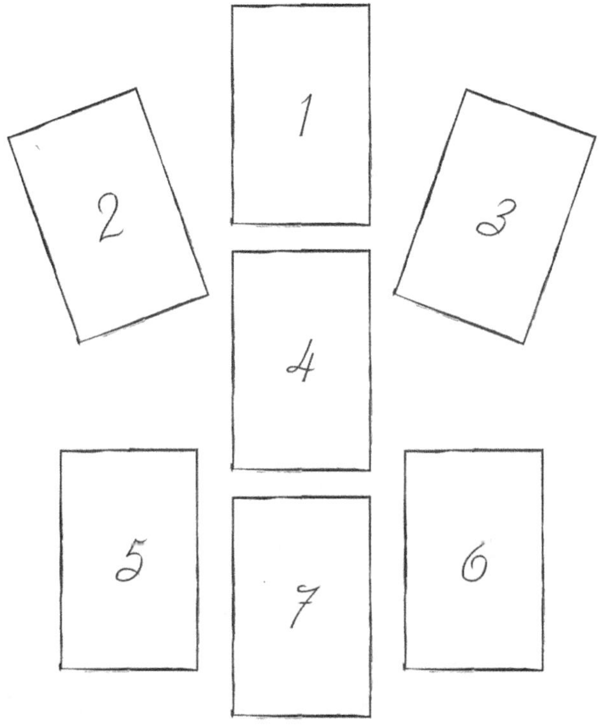

1. Why do I want to invest – my time, money, and/or energy – in this?

2. What do I know about this investment?

3. What don't I know about this investment (yet)?

4. What are the risks involved?

5. Why would this investment be worth these risks?

6. Why wouldn't this investment be worth these risks?

7. What do I have to keep in mind as I make my decision?

Stop

Sometimes, walking away seems to be the only option left, whether we're talking about a project, a collaboration, or a business as a whole. The spreads in this section will help you figure out whether calling it quits is truly the best thing for you right now or whether there's actually something else you need.

39
TAKE A BREAK?

As a relentless workaholic, I've found that taking breaks is not my specialty. I tend to keep going until I'm so wiped out that all I want to do is run away from everything and everyone as fast and as far as I can. Which is exactly why I created this spread, to figure out not only why I'm craving a break but also what I need a break from and how to best go about it.

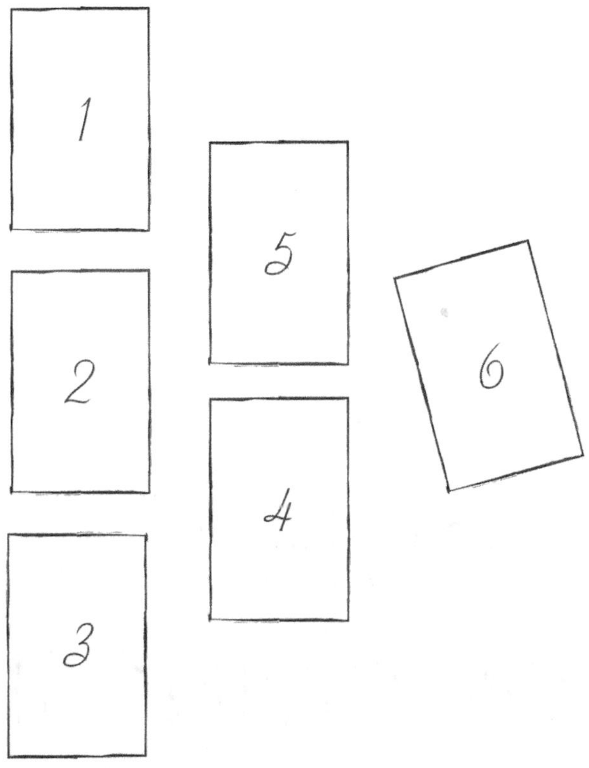

1. Why do I feel as if I'm in need of a break?

2. What exactly do I need a break from?

3. Why do I need a break from this specifically?

4. How can I best take a break from this?

5. How will I know when I'm ready to get back to it?

6. General advice about the situation.

40

GIVING UP
OR GIVING IN

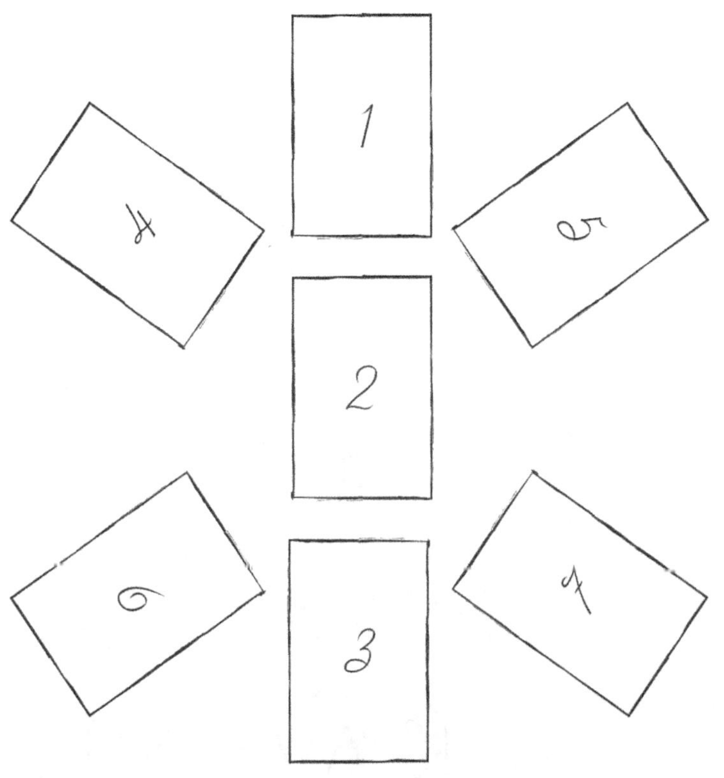

1. Where am I?

2. Where do I want to be?

3. Why aren't I there yet?

4. What is working against me?

5. What is working for me?

6. What if I gave up and stopped trying?

7. What if I gave in and surrendered to what

needs to be done to get me there?

41

IS IT TIME TO
WALK AWAY?

Whether you're thinking of quitting a project, a client, a collaboration, or something else, this spread will help you figure out what's in your best interest right now: to stay or walk away. Keep this one close because you can obviously use this spread for a plethora of non-business situations as well.

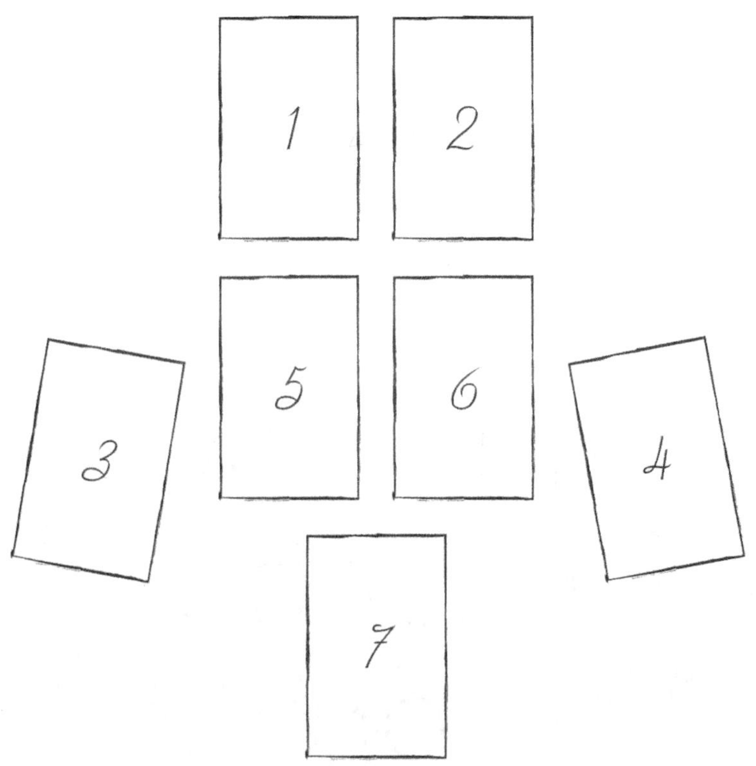

1. What is bothering me about this situation?

2. Why is this bothering me so much?

3. What do I stand to lose by walking away?

4. What do I stand to lose by staying?

5. What do I stand to gain by walking away?

6. What do I stand to gain by staying?

7. General advice on how best to deal with this situation.

42

THE SHOW MUST GO ON

or mustn't it?

Are you a quitter? If yes, great! There's absolutely nothing wrong with knowing when it's time to pack up and move on. After all, not everything is meant to be forever (embrace that Eight of Cups energy!). That said, if you aren't sure whether it's time to call it quits yet, or at all, this spread should be able to provide you with some much-needed clarity.

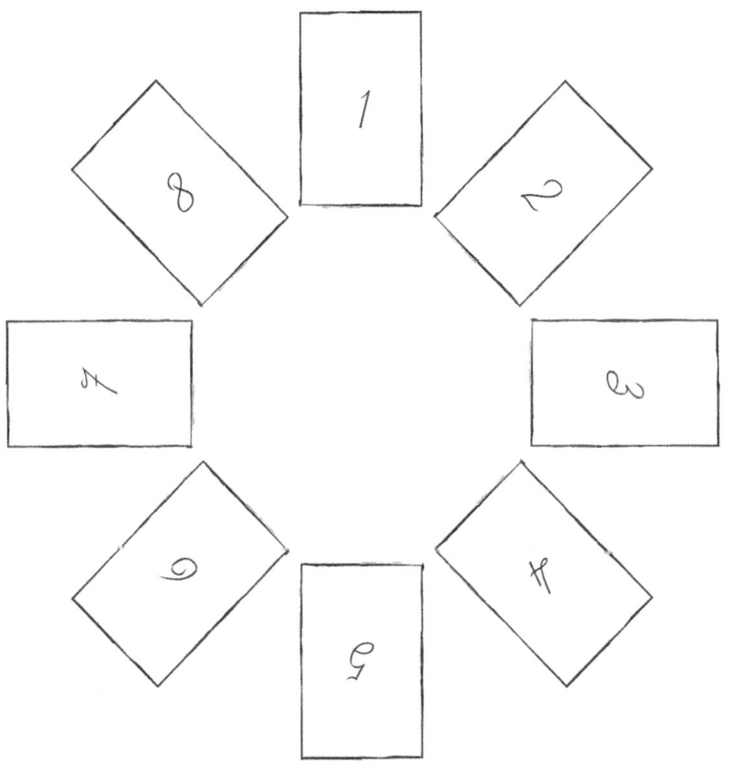

1. How am I currently feeling about my business?

2. Why am I feeling this way?

3. What has caused this feeling?

4. What part do I play in this?

5. What part does my business play in this?

6. What needs to change for me to continue this work?

7. What is the most likely outcome if I step away?

8. What is the most likely outcome if I stay?

Staple

All eight card spreads gathered in this section are business editions of my favourite spreads to keep on hand. All spreads were unlocked during the Kickstarter campaign that funded the publication of this book.

43

THE DAY
AHEAD
SPREAD

business edition

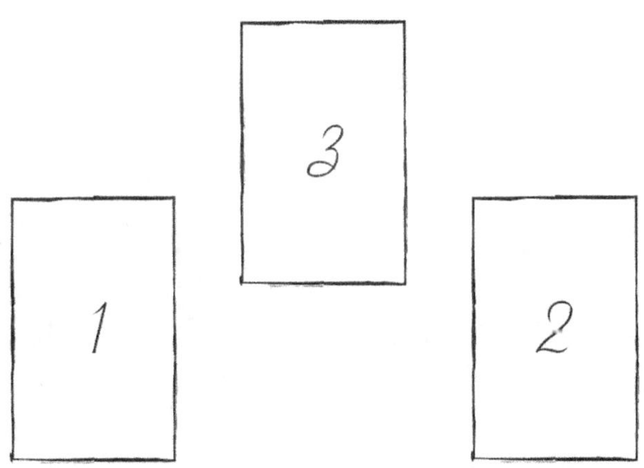

1. What energy surrounds my business today?

2. What energy do I need to bring to my business today?

3. How can I make the absolute best of today's workday?

44

THE WEEK AHEAD SPREAD

business edition

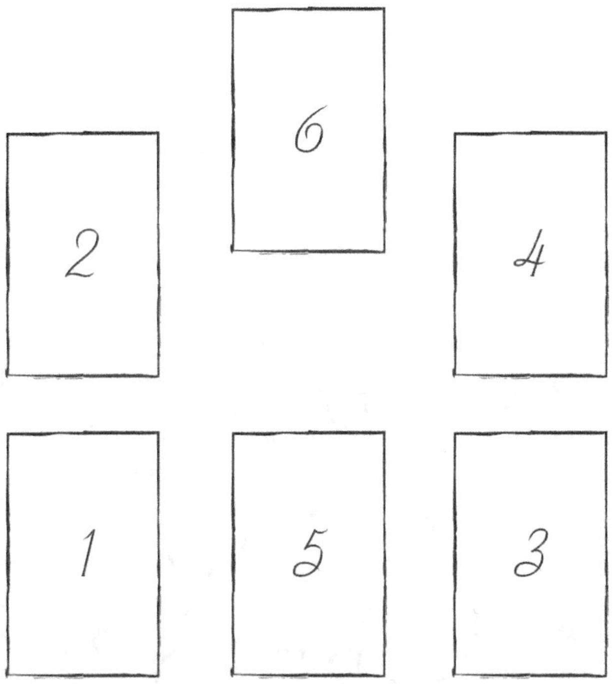

1. What energy surrounds my business this week?

2. What energy do I need to bring to my business this week?

3. What might throw me and/or my business off track this week?

4. If that happens, how do I best stay on track?

5. What other surprises does this week have in store for me

and/or my business?

6. General advice for the upcoming week.

45

THE MONTH AHEAD SPREAD

business edition

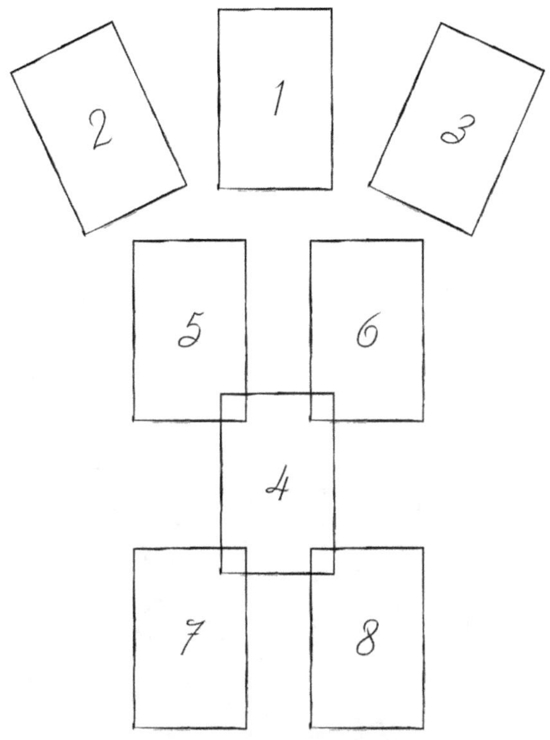

1. What business lessons have I learned over the last month?

2. What about last month do I have to let go of?

3. What about last month should I keep close to my heart?

4. What aspect of my business should I focus my attention on this month?

5. What action(s) should I take this month?

6. What lesson(s) will there be to learn this month?

7. What obstacle(s) will my business and I face this month?

8. How can I best handle these obstacles?

46

THE YEAR
AHEAD
SPREAD

business edition

1. What are my business goals and intentions for the next year?

(Draw up to three cards.)

2. What is the main challenge my business will face during this year (a)

and how can I best go about it (b)?

3. What lesson must I learn during this period to ensure growth?

4. What mindset will help me turn the next year into a success?

5. How can I best prepare for the year ahead?

6. How might other areas of my life affect my business over the next

twelve months?

7. What mustn't I forget about my entrepreneurial self as the next

twelve months unfold?

47

I MADE IT THROUGH THE YEAR SPREAD

*The anniversary spread
–business edition*

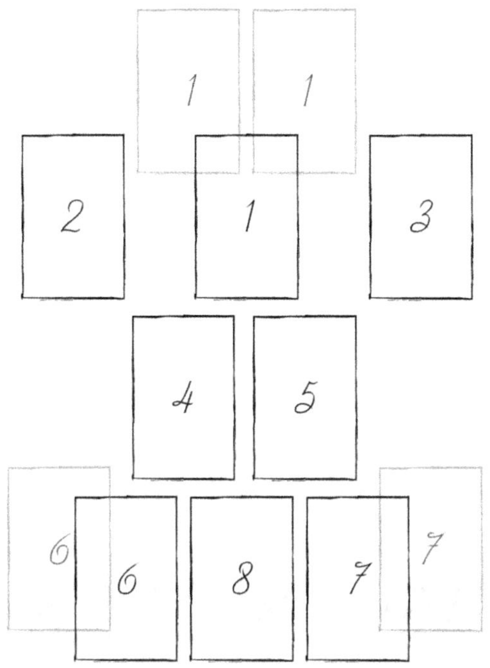

1. What business lessons have I learned over the past twelve months?

(Draw up to three cards.)

2. What do I need to leave behind?

3. What do I need to take with me into the new year?

4. What defined my business purpose last year?

5. What defines my business purpose for the coming year?

6. What business challenges lie ahead?

(Draw up to two cards.)

7. What business opportunities lie ahead?

(Draw up to two cards.)

8. How can I stay true to myself and my business as these obstacles

and opportunities unfold?

48

WHY THIS WORRY?

business edition

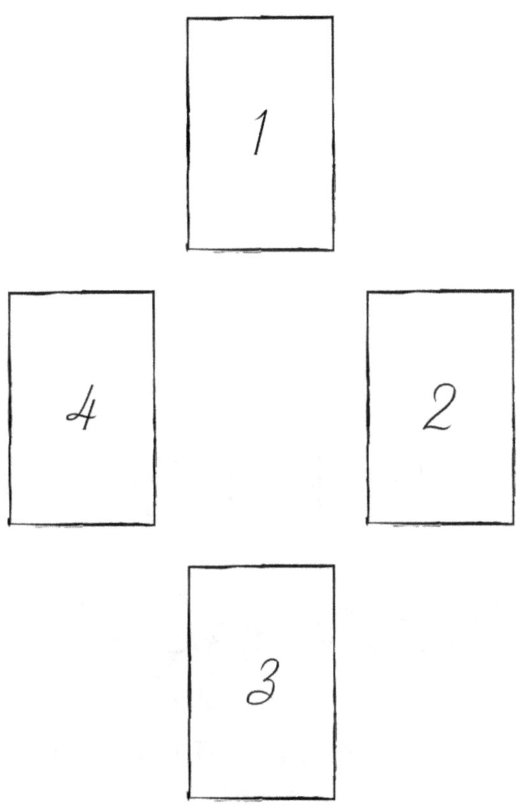

1. What am I worrying about in my business?

2. Where does this worry come from?

3. Why is this worry manifesting right now?

4. What can I do to overcome this worry?

49

HELLO,
NEW DECK!

business edition

Interviewing a new deck is an excellent way to familiarise yourself with the cards and begin a meaningful relationship with them. This business version of an interview spread – which can be used with any deck, old or new – will help you see how your deck(s) might guide your present and future business endeavours specifically.

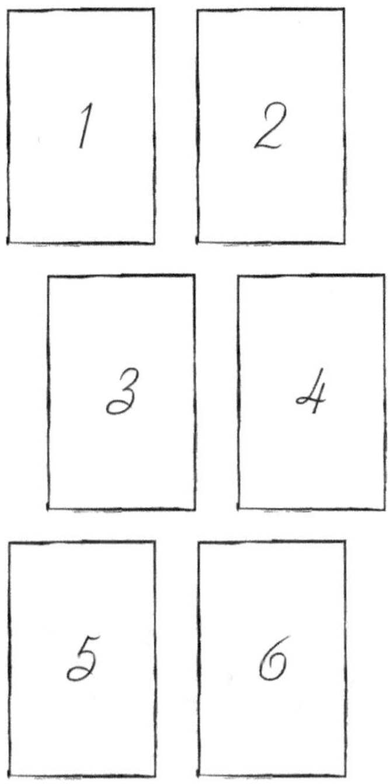

1. What is your biggest strength when it comes to business-related questions?

2. What is your biggest weakness when it comes to business-related questions?

3. How do you see the entrepreneur in me?

4. How might you help me unleash my full entrepreneurial potential?

5. What kind of support might you offer me in my entrepreneurial endeavours?

6. How might you help my business as a whole grow?

50

THE CELTIC CROSS

business edition

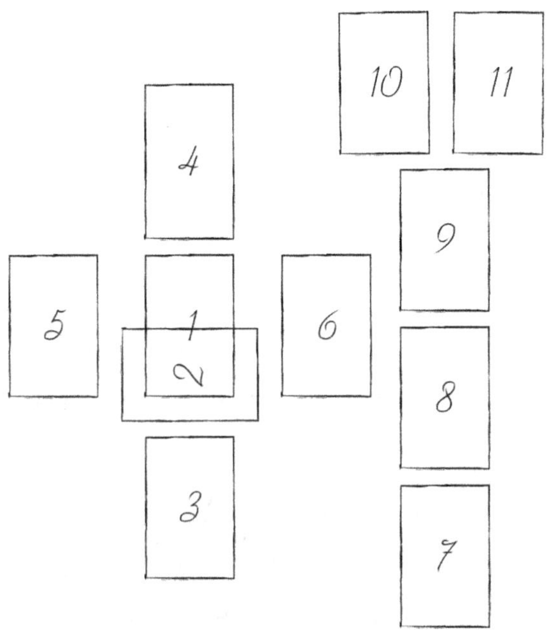

1. What is at the heart of this business matter?

2. What energy surrounds this business matter?

3. What lies at the root of this business matter?

4. What limiting beliefs do I have about this business matter?

5. How have I dealt with similar business matters in the past?

6. What future business matters is this current matter

preparing me for?

7. What is my role in this business matter?

8. What external influences play a role in this business matter?

9. What advice do I need to take to heart?

10. What is the final outcome if I stick to my current course?

11. What is the final outcome if I heed the advice given here?

FIVE QUICK ONE-, TWO-, AND THREE- CARD SPREADS

for entrepreneurs

The list of quick business draws is virtually endless,
but here are some of my go-to mini spreads. I hope
they'll inspire you to ask quick questions of your own.

$$\boxed{\quad 1 \quad}$$

FIVE QUICK ONE-CARD SPREADS

- What energy do I need to bring to work today?

- Who or what might try to throw me off track today?

- What do I need to remember about myself right now?

- What do I need to know about this project/client?

- What makes me the right person for this project/client?

FIVE QUICK TWO-CARD SPREADS

• What valid / invalid fear(s) do I have around this project or client?

• What are the known / unknown aspects of this project?

• What do I love / hate about this project or client?

• What is the most probable outcome if I finish / don't finish

this project?

• What do I want from this project or client? / What will this

project or client give me?

FIVE QUICK THREE-CARD SPREADS

• Where am I now? / Where do I want to be? / How am I going

to get there?

• Where do I want to be? / What is in my way? / How do I

overcome this obstacle?

• What isn't working here? / Why isn't it working? /

How do I solve this?

• What does this client want from me? / What do I want from this

client? / Where is our professional relationship headed?

• What did I do well during this project? / What could I have done

better? / What lesson do I need to take to heart?

CANDLE SPELL FOR SOVEREIGNTY

Use this simple candle spell to invite a sense
of sovereignty into your business.

- Pick a candle. Any colour will work, but keep in mind that certain colours are inclined to invite in certain energies, so pick a white one if you're uncertain. I associate sovereignty with the solar plexus chakra, so I prefer using yellow or golden candles for this spell. Tapered or dinner candles are ideal, but tealights will work too if that's what you have available.

- Take a needle or something else that will allow you to carve the word 'sovereignty' along the side of your candle.

- If you own any essential oils, you might want to use these to anoint your candle. You can pick one of your favourite scents or go with an essential oil that aligns with the energy you're invoking here. For sovereignty, that could be cinnamon, juniper berry, or something citrusy, such as lemon, lime, or orange. Other essential oils you could use for this spell include bergamot for confidence, cedarwood for courage, lavender for tranquillity, or ylang-ylang to lessen anxiety and anger.

- Add a few drops of essential oil to a cotton pad and distribute the oil equally over the candle, avoiding the wick. Make sure to let the oil dry before you light it. When using tealights, be sure not to add too much oil onto the surface (unless you enjoy sparks). To prevent this, you could take the tealight from its holder and anoint the sides before putting it back in.

- Light your candle while reciting the following words or any version of them that resonates with you:

'I call upon the divine Source to bless this candle and so bless me. By lighting this candle, I ask Source to bring the gift that is sovereignty to me for the highest good of all involved.'

- Repeat this invocation three times, ending it with the words 'And so it is.'

- If these exact words don't align with you, rewrite them to fit your own style and intention. You can call upon anyone you feel comfortable with.

- Now let the candle burn down by itself. If you aren't able to let the candle burn down in one go, make sure to snuff it out in between candle-lighting sessions. Blowing a candle out scatters its energy, and that's exactly the opposite of what you're trying to do here. When you relight the candle, don't forget to recite the invocation three times and ending it on 'And so it is.'

This candle spell can also be used to evoke other energies. For example, you could invite in courage, clarity, abundance, harmony, peace, and even your ideal client:

- Pick a white candle or one with an appropriate colour for what you want to invoke.
- Write what you want to invoke down on your candle.
- Anoint it with your favourite or the most fitting essential oils, if you're following this step.
- Reword the invocation on the previous page to fit your intention.

- Light your candle while reciting your reworded invocation and repeating it three times, ending it on 'And so it is.'

135

THE TROLL JAR

because haters gonna hate...

When you spread your wings and take flight, when you step into the light and proudly share your success with the world, you inevitably open yourself up to criticism. This is why the bold energy of the Six of Wands is immediately followed by the confusing and overwhelming energy of the Seven of Wands.

Through visibility we find our audience, but being visible means being seen by more than those who are aligned with you. There will be people who don't care about your message, who are jealous of your success, or who don't think you deserve that kind of success to begin with.

Unfortunately, there's no way around this. Haters are gonna hate, both offline and online, and the more visible and successful you become, the louder the haters are going to be. This is where the troll jar comes in. Because if haters are gonna hate anyway, no matter what we say or do, how about we start taking their presence, their comments, their nastiness for what it truly is? A gauge to measure our success with as well as our bravery and willingness to stand out from the crowd.

Of course, not all criticism calls for the troll jar. Constructive criticism is vital for growth, so it is important to differentiate between comments that are constructive and intended to build you up and make you even better at what you're doing and comments that are purely intended to diminish you, put you down, make you doubt yourself, or urge you to retreat or give up altogether.

Create your own troll jar

- Write down a list of all the things you're scared people might do or say about you. Don't spend too long on this; you can expand the list later.

- Get yourself a jar and decorate it if you're called to do so. I used a gorgeous teal metallic pen to write *Haters gonna hate!* on mine.

- Decide on the amount. I hardly carry cash, so I took a small notepad and wrote €1,- on each page. Each time someone comments in a way that's far from constructive, I fold one of those pages and drop it in my jar.

- Think of a few things you would like to do with the money once your jar is full.

- Be your awesome self and see your jar fill up as you let the haters say whatever they want about you. After all, you know what their words truly signify.

Please note: your jar filling up quickly might not be a sign that you're being absolutely brave and rocking the visibility thing. It could be that you're simply surrounded by people who, for whatever reason, don't see you for who you truly are and don't want you to live up to your potential. If the same people keep making you drop money into your jar, you might need to reconsider your relationship with or closeness to these persons. Could you minimise the time you spend with them or cut them out of your life entirely if you wanted to? Don't think about what others would say about this: it's your life, and if people want to be part of it, they'll have to try harder and be better.

OFFICE CLEARING

Whether you work from home or your workspace is elsewhere, clearing it regularly will keep the energy positive and flowing. If you can't get away with smoke cleansing or misting your workspace, carrying the right kind of crystals with you will go a long way (as will eating lots of oranges).

<h2 style="text-align:center">Smoke cleansing</h2>

The smoke from incense or smudge sticks can be used to clear negative or stagnant energy from your workspace. Different cultures have used different methods and tools to purify their spaces with smoke.

To cleanse with smoke sustainably and in a culturally appropriate way, try to find out how your ancestors cleansed their spaces by using smoke and what material they typically burned. For example, the Celts, my ancestors, made smudge sticks out of herbs such as sage, rosemary, and lavender and often used feathers to waft the smoke in the appropriate direction. I currently live in Cyprus, where sage, rosemary, and lavender grow abundantly, so I don't need to rely on imported smudge sticks that contain white sage or sticks of palo santo.

While cultural practices differ, it's quite common for sound to be included in cleansing rituals, whether through the use of instruments or your own voice, to help set your intention. If you don't own any instruments that work well with this kind of ritual – like drums, gongs, and singing bowls – you can always look up a fitting mantra or prayer online or come up with one yourself. Simply consider what it is you want to clear – for example, negative energy or 'anything that no longer serves me' – and what you want to call in – for example, clarity, harmony, abundance, and so on.

Oranges

On thespruce.com, Anjie Cho lists six smoke-free cleansing methods, including one that uses my all-time favourite essential oil: orange. She offers two methods, one using fresh oranges and one using essential oil.

Fresh oranges

It doesn't get simpler than this: all you need to do to shift the energy in your workspace is to take some fresh orange peels and squeeze them to release their oils into the air. Alternatively, you can put the fresh orange peels in a spray bottle with water to create a mist you can spray around your workspace when the energy needs a little pick-me-up.

Orange essential oil

If you have (sweet) orange essential oil, you can make a quick office mist by mixing twenty to forty drops of oil with water (around three parts) and alcohol or witch hazel (one part) in a 100 ml spray bottle. Don't forget to shake before use.

Crystals

There are many crystals that have attributes that work well within the workspace, from attracting abundance to promoting clear communication to enhancing mental clarity and creativity. Here, I've focused on the crystals that help with negative energies.

Selenite

Because of its purifying qualities, selenite is the number one crystal for any space, and that includes your workspace. In addition, selenite can be used to cleanse other crystals, and it never needs to be cleansed itself.

Black tourmaline

When it comes to negative energies, black tourmaline is one of the most powerful stones to have in your collection. Not only does it block negative energy from entering a space, it also absorbs, cleanses, and transmutes any negative energies that are already present. This is why black tourmaline, in contrast to selenite, needs to be cleaned regularly – for example, with warm, soapy water or with smoke.

One of the six smoke-free cleansing methods Anjie Cho writes about on thespruce.com is a black tourmaline mist. To create a mist for your own workspace, simply add a piece – or multiple small pieces – of black tourmaline to a spray bottle and fill it up with clean water.

Clear quartz

Clear quartz is another great gemstone to keep in your office or have on you while you're working. Clear quartz filters negative energy and it raises your vibration, making you less vulnerable to negative energies to begin with.

Pyrite

While pyrite is often used in the office to attract abundance, it's another gemstone that's great at blocking negative energy. Having pyrite near also keeps us from becoming drained emotionally, which, as with clear quartz, makes us less vulnerable to negative outside influences.

Hematite

Hematite, like black tourmaline, also absorbs negative energies, making it another great gemstone to keep in your workspace. If you spend a lot of time around a computer and other technological gadgets, hematite, much like clear quartz, will also protect you from any harmful waves or radiation coming off your devices.

The Johre symbol

The Johre symbol is an integral part of the Reiki tradition I've been initiated in. No matter which tradition you've been initiated in yourself, if you're a Level 2 or Level 3 Reiki practitioner, you can use this symbol to cleanse any space you wish, including your workspace. Simply draw the symbol – which you can find online – in each corner of the space, asking it to use its white light to cleanse everything in the room.

Starting the Day with Intention

I like to start my days with an intention or mantra that I continue repeating to myself throughout the day, something specific that keeps me in the right headspace. There are multiple ways to arrive at an intention, and I'll use any and all of them depending on my mood and what I think the day is going to bring.

Whatever method you use, make sure to keep it clear, achievable, and positive. In other words, be as specific as you can be, make sure you're not setting any intentions that set you up for inevitable failure, and keep any and all negative wording out of it. You'll also want to repeat your intention regularly. You can write it down on a sticky note that's in your line of vision, turn it into a wallpaper for your computer or phone screen, or even write it on the back of your hand.

You don't have to have a whole ritual around your intention setting – writing it down somewhere and repeating it to yourself is all it takes – but if you want to, here's a quick morning ritual for you.

- Sit down in a quiet spot. If you have an altar, great, but if you don't, any place you can sit for a few moments without being disturbed works.

- Light a candle if you want to – it doesn't matter what kind.

- Repeat your intention to yourself at least three times. If you haven't written it down yet, this is a great moment to do so.

- When you've finished repeating your intention, close your eyes, take a deep breath, and thank yourself for taking a moment to set this intention. If you lit a candle, you can snuff (not blow!) it out now.

If you work from home, I'd suggest doing your morning ritual immediately before you switch to work mode since it'll help the mental transition from being at home to being at work that a commute tends to provide.

Cartomancy

One of my favourite ways to arrive at an intention is by drawing a daily card. No matter the type of cards you work with, they all carry a message that can be turned into an intention. For example, if you draw The Chariot from the tarot, your intention might be 'Today, I'll get as many balls rolling as I can' or 'Today, I'm going full speed ahead.' If you draw, let's say, the Six of Pentacles, you might want to set an intention around giving and receiving in equal measure.

On days when I find it hard to actually formulate an intention, even if the energy of the card I drew speaks to me loudly and clearly, I keep the card on my desk in a spot where I can't miss it so I receive a constant reminder of the kind of energy I'm going for that day.

Another good spot to place the card you drew is your altar, if you have one. On days when I come up with an intention - which I then write out for myself and place somewhere visible - I put the card there instead of directly on my desk.

Connect to your invisible helpers

There are so many deities, (arch)angels, light beings, and other energies you can ask for help. One way to do so is by creating an intention around it. For example, if you have an important meeting coming up, you could ask Archangel Michael for help by repeating the following words to yourself:

'Today, I ask Archangel Michael for strength and protection during this meeting. Dear Archangel Michael, please provide me with strength and protection for as long as I may need it.'

If you're looking for clarity instead, you could turn to Archangel Jeremiel by setting an intention around receiving clarity on the matter. If you need to make an important decision soon and you have no idea which way to go, you could set an intention around Archangel Uriel, who's renowned for their decision-making help.

If pre-Christian archangels aren't your cup of tea, there are many others out there that might work for you, from Quan Yin to Jesus Christ to Saint Germain to Brigid. Which spiritual beings did your ancestors turn to for guidance? Maybe they can do the same for you.

Start from affirmations

We live in the era of affirmation, and affirmations make great foundations for intention setting. One of my favourite affirmations from my Cards for Creative Courage oracle deck is 'Your success is inevitable.' To me, this translates to 'Today, everything is going my way' or 'Today, I'm only allowing constructive thoughts and comments into my space' because that's what I immediately visualise when I hear the words 'Your success is inevitable': someone who won't let anything (or anyone!) get in her way and doesn't waste energy on what's not meant to propel her forwards. See how I translated those two sentiments, which include multiple negative phrasings, into positive intentions?

To give an example from the companion deck to this book, The Sovereign Success Oracle, what would you do with the affirmation 'Nothing changes if I don't change'? How could you turn that into an intention for your day?

Most of us consider change to be scary, no matter how vital it is to our growth. Because of that, I would go with something that invokes the exact opposite of how we usually respond to change, like 'Today, I embrace change' or 'Today, I'm willingly opening myself up to any changes that are for my highest good and that of all involved.'

Intention setting is a practice and, as with all practices, you'll get better at it the more often you do it. Through doing, you'll also figure out what works best for you – whether that's drawing a card, invoking a spiritual being, using affirmations, coming up with your own, or a mix of all the above – and how you prefer to set your intentions in the morning. If this is a new practice for you, I hope you'll give yourself permission and room to find what method fits you best.

WINDING DOWN AFTER WORK

As someone who works from home, I don't have a commute to help me switch hats and unwind after a long day at the office. After all, my office is ten steps removed from my living room. These intentional practices help me with that. That said, even if you do have the time and space between finishing work and arriving home to switch modes, you still might find these practices helpful, especially if you struggle with setting clear boundaries between on-the-clock and off-the-clock you.

Cut your cords

No matter whether you spend your workday at home, in an office building, in a café, or on the road, you inevitably encounter other people and pick up their (negative) energies, whether online or offline. Whatever else you do to unwind after work, it's always a good idea to first cut these cords and release that energy.

Take a cold shower

I know it sounds horrible, but the shock of cold water to our systems helps shake loose and strip negative energy (both others' and our own) so it can wash, literally, down the drain. While it is important to immerse yourself completely, the cold part of your shower need only take ten to fifteen seconds, after which you can turn the heat up to something much more pleasant.

I much prefer visualisation over taking a cold shower any day, but washing with cold water is the most effective way I know of – and it does feel amazing, once I can breathe again.

Visualisation

Another way to clear any negative energy you've picked up during the day is by visualising the energy leaving your body.

One way to do this is by visualising what colour your own energy has and taking note of all the other colours you see in and around you. Once you've established what is yours and what is not, you can visualise how the other colours are leaving your body to return to the centre of the earth.

Another visualisation technique is to visualise any and all (negative) cords between you and the people you've interacted with today (from the barista who made your drink to the client(s) you had a meeting with). With your weapon of choice – a sword, an axe, a blowtorch, a pair of scissors, a knife, etc. – cut through these cords until they disappear. If your cords disintegrate instead of disappear, visualise all remnants returning to the centre of the earth.

Count your blessings

Gratitude is one of the highest vibrational frequencies a human being can be at. No matter what the day has thrown at you, ending it with gratitude is a great – and quick! – way to recalibrate.

If you don't already practise gratitude, a simple way to incorporate it into your after-work ritual is by writing down three things you are grateful for when looking back on your workday. These don't have to be big things, so there's no need to overthink it. Just make sure to truly feel grateful for whatever it is you write down.

If you want to deepen your practice, you could answer the following two questions next:

- What do I want to remember about today?
- What could I have been more grateful for today?

(Re)Condition your brain

As an entrepreneur, I know that, on any given day, it's easy to feel as if I didn't do enough, that I didn't give my all, that I could've done better, and that I could've done more. Living in a society where your worth is measured against your productivity will do that to you.

Lucky for us, our brains are extremely flexible, and it is possible to reprogramme such intrusive, and dangerous, thoughts. That said, if you've ever tried countering these thoughts, you know how hard it can be to ingrain new, healthier thoughts and how important repetition is in the process.

You can use any positive and empowering counterthought that works for your specific situation. At the end of my own after-work ritual, I like to remind myself that I've done all I could and that it's more than enough by repeating what I consider one of Brené

Brown's most powerful phrases:

'No matter what gets done and how much is left undone, I am enough.'

Depending on how bad my day was, I might not believe it every time, but I know that, the more often I repeat it to myself, the sooner my brain will favour it over those intrusive thoughts that aren't even my own.

CRYSTAL PROGRAMMING

All crystals, or gemstones, have natural properties that will help you no matter what. By programming our crystals, we activate these inherent energies, which allows us to strengthen these energies and/or direct them in a particular direction.

- Pick a crystal whose natural properties are already aligned with what you're trying to manifest. If you're attracting abundance, citrine, tiger's eye, or emerald are always a good choice. If you're seeking harmony in one of your business relations, you might want to go with blue lace agate or blue chalcedony. Figure out what it is exactly you want to achieve and then look for a crystal that matches that goal.

- Set your intention – remember to be clear, achievable, and positive – and write it down so you can easily repeat it while programming your crystal.

- Quiet your mind as best as you can while you hold the crystal you picked in your hand.

- Close or relax your eyes and visualise your intention becoming reality. What do you see? How does it feel?

- Repeat your intention as often as you like. Three is always a good number, but you can repeat it more often if that feels right in the moment.

Don't forget to thank your crystal for helping you achieve what's for the highest good of all. If you can, carry the stone around with you for as long as needed. If your crystal is too big to carry around all day, keep it as close as you can or put it in a significant spot, such as on your altar or desk.

Once you've programmed your crystal, it should be good to go for a while. However, if it starts to feel heavy or dull to you, cleanse and then reprogramme it.

PENDULUM CHARTS

Most card systems, including the tarot, don't respond well to 'Yes' or 'No' questions. This is where pendulum dowsing comes in, a great divination tool that's direct and leaves very little room for interpretation.

To dowse with a pendulum, you'll be needing a... pendulum! That's right. Your local metaphysical shop might sell pendulums, but if you're a crystal hoarder like me, you might be able to create your own: any crystal that ends in a point and can be attached to a piece of string or chain will do.

My 'pendulum' is an amethyst point I originally bought as a pendant. I still wear it around my neck from time to time, but since I started pendulum dowsing, I've mostly been using it as a pendulum.

- Now that you have your pendulum, you need to first figure out which swinging direction – left to right, back and forth, clockwise, or counterclockwise – means what. Mine always swings in the exact same way, but I still double-check it every time I set out to use my pendulum. Simply ask your pendulum the following questions and see which way it swings:

  o What means 'Yes'?
  o What means 'No'?
  o What means 'Maybe'?
  o What means 'I don't know'?

- When using pendulum charts like the ones in this book, the chart determines which direction means what so there's no need to ask your pendulum which way it'll swing for 'Yes', 'No', etc.

- Before you start asking your actual questions, try out a couple of questions you already know the answer to, such as 'Is my car red?', 'Is my cat called Rufus?', or 'Is my mother's name Julia?' Once you're confident your pendulum swings in the right direction for each answer, you can start asking some real questions.*

- Whatever comes up for you, don't second-guess yourself. Accept the answer you've been given for what it is, even if it's the last thing you want to hear right now. The more you distrust your pendulum dowsing, the less accurate your readings will become.

*If your pendulum doesn't move at all after you've asked your question, check in with yourself whether you're truly ready to know the answer. If yes, you might not be grounded and centred enough. Clear your head as best as you can, take a couple of calming breaths, and ask your question again.

What do I do now?

When you're uncertain on how best to respond to a business situation, this chart will help you figure out what your next step of action is. Is it time to jump in without another doubt, to decline, to demand more, or to accept the situation for what it is?

You can download a printable version of this chart at

mswordsmith.nl/tarotforentrepreneursplus.

AT THIS RATE...

Setting the right price for your offerings might be one of the hardest things an entrepreneur ever has to do, which is why I thought you wouldn't mind some help. Use this chart to establish whether the rate you have in mind is just right, or whether you need to change it.

You can download a printable version of this chart at mswordsmith.nl/tarotforentrepreneursplus.

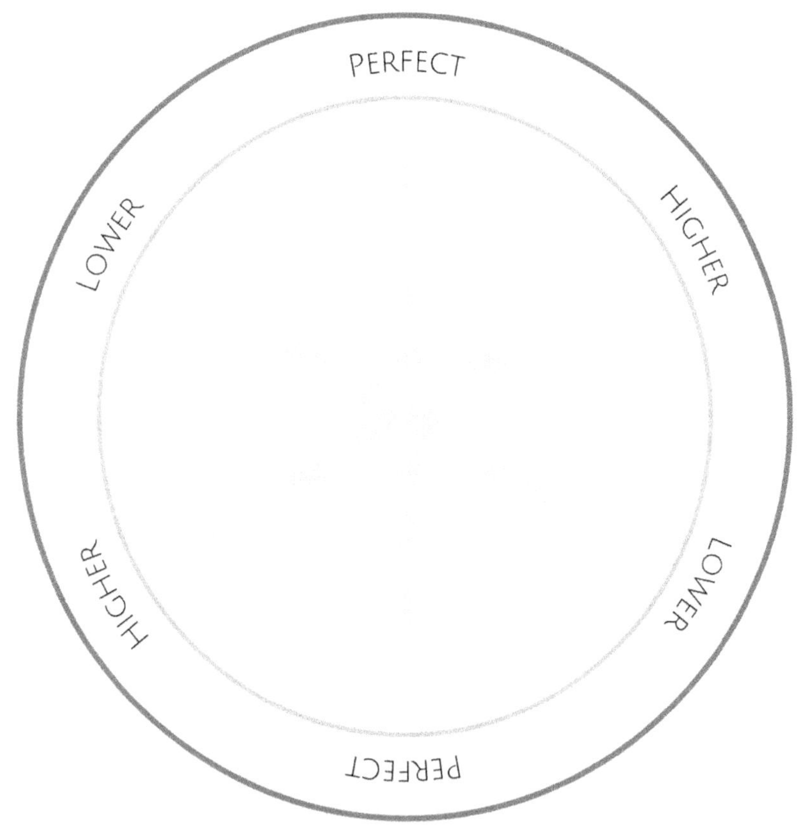

'TIS THE SEASON

I love planning ahead, but I sometimes struggle with figuring out when's the best time to plan for this or that. This chart will help you pinpoint which season's best for whatever you have planned.

You can download a printable version of this chart at

mswordsmith.nl/tarotforentrepreneursplus.

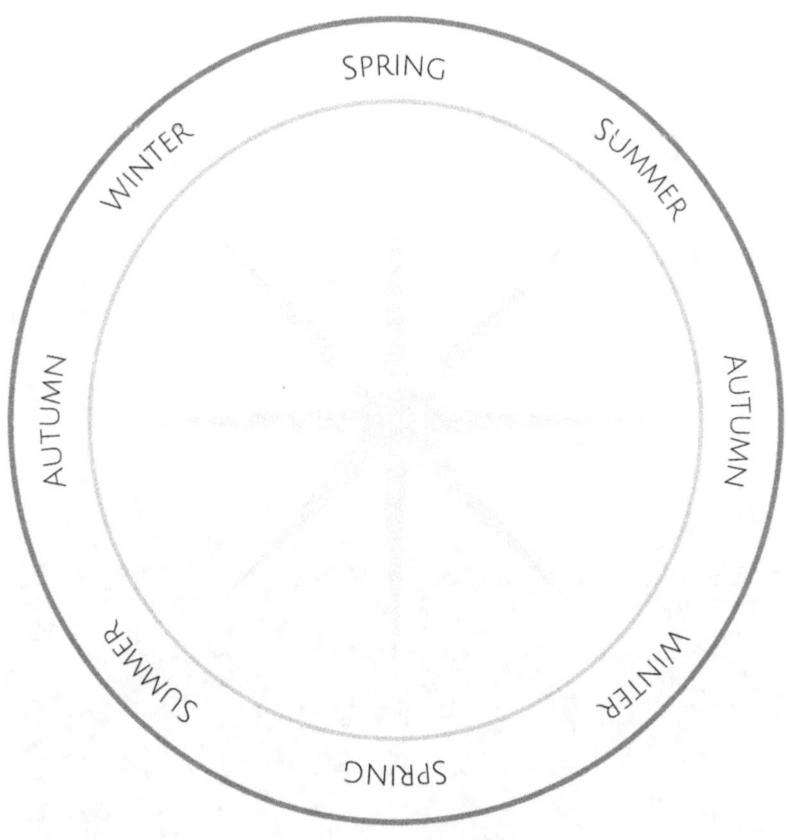

IF NOT NOW, WHEN?

This chart can work with any timeframe as long as you've already established one:

'Should I do X at the beginning, in the middle, or at the end of the day?' 'Should I do Y

at the beginning, in the middle, or near the end of the month?' 'Should I do Z during

the first month, the second month, or the third month of the quarter/season?'

You can download a printable version of this chart at

mswordsmith.nl/tarotforentrepreneursplus.

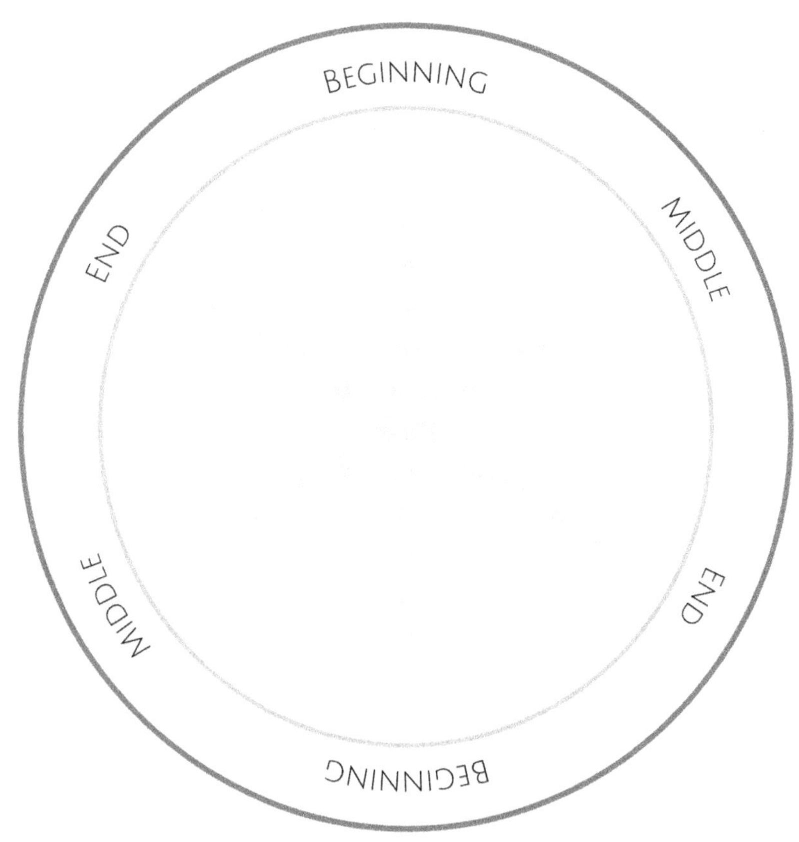

PLEASE CONSIDER LEAVING A REVIEW

Authors are nowhere without honest reviews, and I'd truly appreciate it if you left one on Goodreads, my Facebook page facebook.com/mswordsmith, or the retailer where you bought this book.

THE CREATIVE CARDSLINGERS

ISN'T IT BETTER TO SLING CARDS TOGETHER?

Join my private Facebook group The Creative Cardslingers (password **BLUE APATITE**) to meet fellow creative cardreaders, be the first to test my latest card spreads, and hear all about the creative projects I'm involved in.

AUTHOR'S NOTE

I'm a freelance writer, editor, and writing coach with nearly a decade of experience as an entrepreneur. In 2019, I moved to Cyprus to fully commit to my writing, editing, and coaching business, and it was here that I started working on my first tarot book: *Get Out of Your Own Way*.

By the end of 2019, I had published three more tarot books: *Tarot for Creatives*, *Fleshing Out the Narrative*, and *Set Yourself Up for Success*. In addition, I'd begun drafting a couple of card spreads for the book that would eventually become *Tarot for Entrepreneurs*.

Transitioning into being a full-time entrepreneur increased my need for card spreads that specifically spoke to business-related questions and challenges; however, it also pulled me away from the project since running a full-time business required significant attention. Although I managed to add a spread here and there, I struggled to find the right moment to fully devote myself to the book.

Even then, I sensed that this particular collection of spreads would surpass any of the tarot books I'd previously created. This realisation made the project seem rather daunting, especially given my limited time and energy over the past few years. While I did publish some tarot-related work at the beginning of the pandemic, when I still had enough drive and stamina to create, I was far from ready to truly dive into this book.

In early 2023, *Tarot for Entrepreneurs* resurfaced in my thoughts. For the first time since the pandemic, I felt the timing was right to finish it. I picked a target date, decided to launch it through Kickstarter for some extra accountability, and set to work.

And now, almost four years since its inception, the book is here.

If the spreads and other intentional practices included within are only half as beneficial to you as they've been to me, then I am thrilled to finally get to share them with the rest of the world.

If you want to get in touch or know what I'm up to, there are different ways and places to contact and follow me:

Website: mswordsmith.nl
Newsletter: mswordsmith.nl/newsletter
E-mail: marielle@mswordsmith.nl
Instagram: mariellessmith
Instagram: tarotforcreatives
Facebook: mswordsmith

Acknowledgements

The publication of this book would not have been possible without the support of those who backed my *Tarot for Entrepreneurs* Kickstarter campaign. My eternal gratitude goes out to the following people and every backer who wished to remain anonymous:

Myriam, Ember Kley Taylor, Lisa Kelly-Mulhern, Winnie, Viannah E. Duncan, Michelle Blanchard, DY, Amy Teegan, Clarissa Gosling, Stefanie Peeters, Joanne Wolf, Bethany Tucker, Alma Noir, Tammy Sanders, Karen Guyler, Pamela Cummins, Kenneth E Baker, Saleh M. Abdullah, Loren Morris, Ashlie Wittenmyer, Amy Dunaway, Miranda Forner, Nijeara "Ny" Buie, Billy Jo Ayakatubby, Tanya Michelle, Lee Nielsen, Eddy Pierre, Melri Nightwind, Derek Murphy, Cheenah, Wendy Sánchez, Kate Sheeran Swed, Jimmy Ray Tyner 3rd, Emily Rousell, Mary Collin, Linda Rodríguez, Maria A.

I truly can't thank you enough for making my dreams happen.

I'd also like to thank Andri for embracing me the way I am and putting up with my writerly shenanigans. One day, I promise you, I'll be better at planning around big deadlines.